DK EYEWITNESS

P9-CSW-809

TOP 10
ST PETERSBURG

Top 10 St Petersburg Highlights

The Top 10 of Everything

CONTENTS

St Petersburg Area by Area

Streetsmart

Within each Top 10 list in this book, no hierarchy of quality or popularity is implied. All 10 are, in the editor's opinion, of roughly equal merit.

Title page, front cover and spine Colourful domes and mosaics on the Church on Spilled Blood
Back cover, clockwise from top left Catherine Palace; Summer Garden; Winter Canal; Church on Spilled Blood; Winter Palace

Welcome to
St Petersburg

Packed with magnificent palaces, Russia's second city exudes the irresistible splendour of its imperial past. World-class restaurants, a vibrant nightlife, cutting-edge modern art galleries and some of the world's most spectacular museums are among its many attractions. With Eyewitness Top 10 St Petersburg, it's yours to explore.

Aptly known as the "Venice of the North", St Petersburg is a city of canals, bridges, plazas and narrow passageways. It is best explored by boat or on foot, despite it having one of the deepest metro systems in the world. The city centre's fine Baroque and Neo-Classical buildings are remarkably well preserved, and its cathedrals and churches are stunning. Peter the Great's splendid summer residence at **Peterhof** is a short boat ride away and the sumptuous Romanov palaces of **Tsarskoe Selo** and **Pavlovsk** lie just beyond the city limits.

Though renowned for fine Russian restaurants serving traditional dishes in palatial surroundings, you'll find the city's broad choice of eateries includes raw vegan cafés, steakhouses and innovative fusion cuisine. Exhibitions and performances are held throughout the year, but St Petersburg's cultural peak occurs during the brief weeks of the **White Nights**, when the sun barely sets and thousands of tourists join exuberant locals for back-to-back festivals and events.

Whether you're visiting for a weekend or a week, our Top 10 guide describes the best of everything that St Petersburg has to offer, from the **Hermitage's** highlights, to the scattered palaces of the Romanov dynasty. The guide has useful tips throughout, from seeking out what's free to avoiding the crowds, plus eight easy-to-follow itineraries designed to tie together a clutch of sights in a short space of time. Add inspiring photography and detailed maps, and you've got the essential pocket-sized travel companion. **Enjoy the book, and enjoy St Petersburg**.

Clockwise from top: **Church on Spilled Blood and the Russian Museum; Catherine Palace, Tsarskoe Selo; columns of the Cathedral of Our Lady of Kazan; the Main Staircase at the Winter Palace;** *matryoshki* **(nesting dolls); a city canal; Cameron Gallery, Tsarskoe Selo**

Exploring St Petersburg

For things to see and do, visitors to St Petersburg are spoiled for choice. Whether here for just a weekend or longer, here are some ideas for two and four days of sightseeing in this magnificent city.

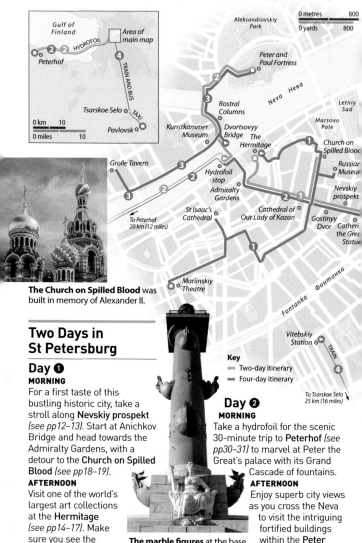

The Church on Spilled Blood was built in memory of Alexander II.

The marble figures at the base of the Rostral Columns represent Russian rivers.

Two Days in St Petersburg

Day ❶

MORNING

For a first taste of this bustling historic city, take a stroll along **Nevskiy prospekt** (see pp12–13). Start at Anichkov Bridge and head towards the Admiralty Gardens, with a detour to the **Church on Spilled Blood** (see pp18–19).

AFTERNOON

Visit one of the world's largest art collections at the **Hermitage** (see pp14–17). Make sure you see the spectacular Winter Palace State Rooms.

Key

━━ Two-day itinerary
━━ Four-day itinerary

Day ❷

MORNING

Take a hydrofoil for the scenic 30-minute trip to **Peterhof** (see pp30–31) to marvel at Peter the Great's palace with its Grand Cascade of fountains.

AFTERNOON

Enjoy superb city views as you cross the Neva to visit the intriguing fortified buildings within the **Peter and Paul Fortress** (see pp24–5).

The Hermitage contains the former Winter Palace and its State Rooms.

Four Days in St Petersburg

Day ❶

MORNING
Head for the opulent buildings of the **Hermitage** (see pp14–17) to admire its sublime 18th-century architecture and explore its world-class art collection.

AFTERNOON
Consider remaining at the Hermitage for the rest of the afternoon, or visit the nearby **St Isaac's Cathedral** (see pp28–9) and the **Russian Museum** (see pp22–3). Afterwards, catch an evening performance at the **Mariinskiy Theatre** (see pp20–21).

Day ❷

MORNING
Walk along **Nevskiy prospekt** (see pp12–13), the main street since the city was founded. Look out for Catherine the Great's statue, **Gostinyy Dvor** mall (see p61) and the **Cathedral of Our Lady of Kazan** (see p68).

AFTERNOON
The magnificent gardens and palaces of **Peterfof** (see pp30–31) are just a 30-minute hydrofoil ride from the Hermitage Embankment. Don't miss the Grand Cascade, the Great Palace's main staircase and the Throne Room.

Day ❸

MORNING
From the **Hermitage** (see pp14–17), cross Dvortsovyy Bridge to visit Strelka, the historic quarter of **Vasilevskiy Island** (see pp88–91) famous for the **Kunstkammer Museum** (see p89) and the **Rostral Columns** (see p89).

AFTERNOON
Lunch at the lively **Grolle Tavern** (see p93) before crossing Birzhevoy Bridge to see the **Peter and Paul Fortress** (see pp24–5), where the tombs of the Romanovs are contained within the Baroque Cathedral of SS Peter and Paul.

Day ❹

MORNING
Start early for a trip to the stunning palaces at **Tsarskoe Selo** (see pp32–3). Don't miss the Amber Room and the Great Hall.

AFTERNOON
Take a taxi to the wonderful palace and gardens of **Pavlovsk** (see pp34–5) to the southeast of the city.

Catherine Palace, at Tsarskoe Selo, was the summer residence of the tsars.

○ Anichkov Bridge

Top 10 St Petersburg Highlights

**The Grand Cascade in front of the
Great Palace, Peterhof**

🔟 St Petersburg Highlights

From the pre-revolutionary grandeur of the Hermitage to the ubiquitous reminders of the country's Soviet period, St Petersburg is a city where eras and architectural styles collide. Blessed with magnificent skylines, the city has been the inspiration for many of Russia's greatest writers, from Gogol to Dostoevsky. Known as "The Venice of the North", Russia's second city is a place of wonder and enigma.

1 Nevskiy Prospekt
The cultural heart of the city is home to many top sights, including the Cathedral of Our Lady of Kazan *(see p68)*.

2 The Hermitage
This opulent former residence of the tsars has one of the world's largest art collections, with masterpieces by Leonardo da Vinci and Michelangelo *(see pp14–17)*.

3 Church on Spilled Blood
The twisted, colourful domes of this church make it one of the city's most famous landmarks *(see pp18–19)*.

4 Mariinskiy Theatre
World-class ballet and opera can be seen at the Mariinskiy Theatre, the Mariinskiy II and the Concert Hall *(see pp20–21)*.

5 Russian Museum
This museum features a wide range of Russian art, including the works of Bryullov and Repin *(see pp22–3)*.

6 Peter and Paul Fortress
The history of the city dates from the founding of the fortress in 1703. It was originally intended to defend the city against Swedish invaders *(see pp24–5)*.

7 St Isaac's Cathedral
The largest church in Russia took 40 years to complete. Its interior ceiling paintings survived shelling during World War II *(see pp28–9)*.

8 Peterhof
With its Great Palace and magnificent landscaped gardens, Peterhof encapsulates the extravagance of tsarist Russia. Located 30 km (19 miles) west of the city, it is an ideal day trip *(see pp30–31)*.

9 Tsarskoe Selo
A fine example of tsarist architectural splendour, Tsarskoe Selo, with its lavish imperial palace and beautiful parks, is the perfect place to spend a relaxing day *(see pp32–3)*.

10 Pavlovsk
In 1777, Catherine the Great presented Pavlovsk to her son, the future tsar Paul I. Today it is a romantic cluster of ruins around a charming palace *(see pp34–5)*.

🔟 ⭐ Nevskiy Prospekt

A stroll along Nevskiy prospekt is a journey through time, from tsarist-era splendours to the cafés and chic boutiques of modern-day St Petersburg. Immortalized in Russian literature, this 4.5-km (3-mile) stretch has been the hub of the city's social life since the 18th century. Home to numerous fine churches and monuments, this is an ideal starting point for an exploration of the city. Many of St Petersburg's most famous sights, such as the unforgettable Cathedral of Our Lady of Kazan, are just a short walk away.

3 Russian National Library

Russia's oldest state library houses around 33 million items, and also boasts the oldest handwritten book in the Russian language, which dates from 1057 **(left)**.

1 Catherine the Great's Statue

Catherine the Great *(see p16)* was a German princess who came to power in Russia after an imperial coup in 1762, during which her husband, Peter III, was murdered. This is the only statue of her in St Petersburg.

2 Beloselskiy-Belozerskiy Palace

The Beloselskiy-Belozerskiy Palace, housing offices and a concert hall, was once home to one of Rasputin's murderers *(see p80)*. It later served as the Soviet-era headquarters of the Communist Party.

4 Gogol Statue

Many of Nikolai Gogol's stories *(see p46)* are set in the city. This statue (1997), by Mikhail Belov, is a fitting tribute to his troubled genius.

5 Armenian Church

This pretty church (1780) **(above)** was designed by the court architect of Catherine the Great, Yuriy Velten. A ruin *(see p67)* during the Soviet period, the "Blue Pearl of Nevskiy prospekt" now serves the Armenian community.

NEED TO KNOW

MAP L3–P4 ■ www.nevsky-prospekt.com

Beloselskiy-Belozerskiy Palace: Tours by appointment; open for concerts

Russian National Library: open 9am–9pm Mon–Fri, 11am–7pm Sat & Sun

Armenian Church: open 9am–8pm

Cathedral of Our Lady of Kazan: open 8:30am–end of evening service (from 6:30am Sat & Sun)

Gostinyy Dvor: open 10am–10pm

Church of St Catherine: open 9am–9pm

Stroganov Palace Russian Museum: open 10am–6pm Mon (to 6pm Wed & Fri–Sun), 1–9pm Thu; adm adults ₽350; students ₽170

■ There is a lot of heavy traffic on Nevskiy prospekt, and pedestrians should use the *perekhodi* – crosswalks or the underpass – in the central part of the avenue. The underpass is indicated by street signs showing a flight of steps.

Map of Nevskiy Prospekt

7 Gostinyy Dvor

This striking columned arcade *(see p61)* has been the focal point of the city's shopping since the mid-18th century. It houses a vast array of shops.

8 Church of St Catherine

The oldest Roman Catholic church in Russia *(see p69)*. An 18th-century mixture of Baroque and Neo-Classical styles, the structure can hold up to 2,500 people.

9 Siege Plaque

Dating from the years of the World War II siege of the city *(see p38)*, the plaque reads, "Citizens! This side of the street is more dangerous during an artillery bombardment!"

10 Stroganov Palace

This Baroque-style palace **(below)** *(see pp22–3)* once had an exhibition devoted to the evils of the aristocracy. The building now belongs to the Russian Museum.

6 Cathedral of Our Lady of Kazan

The 1811 cathedral **(above)** *(see p68)* was inspired by St Peter's Basilica in Rome. Used as a museum of atheism during the Soviet period, religious services made a return in 1992.

🔟⭐ The Hermitage

This grand ensemble of buildings on the bank of the Neva river houses one of the world's greatest art collections. Built up by successive tsars, the museum boasts masterpieces by Picasso and Rembrandt, as well as prehistoric, Classical and Oriental art exhibits. It also contains the Winter Palace, the pre-revolutionary residence of the tsars and headquarters for the Provisional Government after the 1917 Revolution. It's said that it would take 11 years to examine every one of the Hermitage's exhibits.

1 Palace Square
This imposing square **(below)**, designed by Carlo Rossi, overlooks the Hermitage's main entrance and was the setting for the Bloody Sunday massacre of 1905 *(see p38)*.

2 Winter Palace
The opulent Winter Palace was built for Tsarina Elizabeth between 1754 and 1762. It contains the magnificent Malachite Room, decorated with over two tonnes of ornamental stone, and architect Francesco Bartolomeo Rastrelli's masterpiece, the Main Staircase.

3 General Staff Building
The Impressionist and Post-Impressionist collection has moved to new galleries within this 19th-century building.

4 Atlantes
Ten 5-m- (16-ft-) tall granite Atlantes **(above)** prop up the Hermitage's former public entrance. A tradition is to rub the toe of one and make a wish.

5 Raphael Loggias
This corridor **(below)** is a copy of the Vatican's famous 16th-century gallery, with 52 chronological biblical scenes.

6 Winter Palace State Rooms

These rooms **(above)** were designed for state ceremonies. The St George Hall is used for state meetings today.

8 Alexander Column

This column is the world's largest freestanding monument. Dedicated to Alexander I, it was erected in 1834.

THE HERMITAGE UNDER SIEGE

The Hermitage came under frequent attack during the World War II siege *(see p38)*. The Nazis pledged to "completely destroy Leningrad" (as St Petersburg was then known), and the Hermitage soon became a symbol of the city's resistance. Although many museum workers died of starvation, and snow piled up inside its halls, the Hermitage continued to support the city's cultural life.

10 The Old Hermitage

Designed by Yuriy Velten, the Old Hermitage was built between 1771 and 1787 to house Catherine the Great's collection of paintings. It was opened as a public museum by Nicholas I in 1852.

7 Pavilion Hall

A gold and white hall with marble columns and crystal chandeliers. It houses James Cox's Peacock Clock, once owned by Prince Grigory Potemkin, Catherine the Great's secret husband.

9 The New Hermitage

The New Hermitage was specifically designed as a museum because of Nicholas I's desire to make the exhibits more accessible to the public.

Plan of The Hermitage

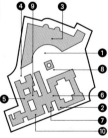

Hermitage Works of Art

1 Madonna Litta
Leonardo da Vinci's *Madonna Litta* (c.1491) is a powerful work that was often copied by his peers. It is one of two paintings by the artist in this museum, the other being *Benois Madonna*.

2 Abraham's Sacrifice
This masterpiece painted by Rembrandt in 1635 depicts the dramatic moment in the Old Testament when an angel prevents Abraham from sacrificing his son to God.

3 Bacchus
Painted by Peter Paul Rubens, *Bacchus* (1638–40) depicts the Roman god of wine and intoxication as a bloated, obese man, wholly abandoned to his own pleasure. The painting was part of a private collection acquired by the Hermitage in 1772.

4 St John the Divine in Silence
A rare example of Russian art in the Hermitage, this icon (1679) was created by a painter from the Kirillo-Byelozyorsk monastery in Arkhangelsk. It depicts St John in deep contemplation of the Bible with his hand touching his lips – a

CATHERINE THE GREAT

Catherine the Great (**above**), a self-confessed "glutton for art", came to power in Russia in 1762. In 1764, she made the first significant purchases for the Hermitage. This initial batch – 225 works of European art bought from a German merchant – is regarded as the birth of the Hermitage as an art gallery. Bulk purchases of art became the norm, as Russian ambassadors and envoys were ordered to build up the collection, buying from impoverished English, Italian and Dutch aristocratic families. The tsarina's personal favourites were works by Rubens and Leonardo.

sign that he is keeping silence in accordance with his holy vow. The icon's date and place of creation is recorded on its reverse.

5 Three Women
Picasso's *Three Women* (1908) is a precursor to the Cubist style that developed in France between 1908 and 1914. There is a distinct African influence in the bold use of colour and the faces of the women, which are inspired by tribal masks.

6 Music
Music was created by Henri Matisse in 1910 for Sergey Shchukin's Moscow mansion. The painting depicts bright red figures, and was denounced at the time as barbaric due to its evocative rendering of abandonment and spontaneity.

St John the Divine in Silence

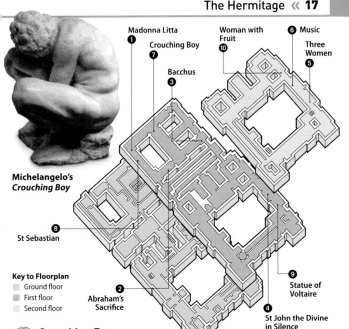

Michelangelo's
Crouching Boy

St Sebastian

Key to Floorplan
  Ground floor
  First floor
  Second floor

Madonna Litta ❶

Crouching Boy ❼

Bacchus ❸

Woman with Fruit ❿

Music ❻

Three Women ❺

❽

Abraham's Sacrifice ❷

❾ Statue of Voltaire

❹ St John the Divine in Silence

The Hermitage Floorplan

❼ Crouching Boy

The meaning of Michelangelo's marble sculpture has been a source of contention among scholars over the years. Some believe the figure is a grieving man or a conquered soldier, others say that it represents a soul yet to be born. Whatever its meaning, there is no denying the energy contained in the figure's evocative pose.

❽ St Sebastian

St Sebastian was painted by Titian in 1576, towards the end of his life, when he produced what are widely considered to be his most moving works. He applied the paint with his fingers or a palette knife and this, coupled with the deep colours he used, produces a dramatic effect.

❾ Statue of Voltaire

The statue of Voltaire dates from 1781, and is Jean-Antoine Houdon's most famous work, sculpted from life studies when Voltaire visited Paris in 1778. The lifelike face of the philosopher shows a remarkable depth of characterization.

Woman with Fruit

❿ Woman with Fruit

This painting is representative of Gauguin's work during his stay in the French Polynesian Islands in the 1890s. The bright colours and flowing lines evoke a tropical paradise – some say the work symbolizes Eve in the Garden of Eden.

★ Church on Spilled Blood

The Church on Spilled Blood, a cacophony of colour just off Nevskiy prospekt, stands out in St Petersburg by nature of its Russian Revival style, something that is extremely rare in this city of Baroque and Neo-Classical architecture. Designed by Alfred Parland and Ignatiy Malyshev, the church, sometimes referred to as "Saviour on Blood", was built as a memorial to Alexander II in 1881 on the site of his assassination. The sanctuary doors covered in semi-precious stones are particularly awe-inspiring.

3 Mosaic Walls
The church has more than 7,000 sq m (75,300 sq ft) of mosaics, both on the interior and exterior. Materials such as jasper, porphyry and marble were used to create these lavish artworks **(right)**.

1 Mosaic Portraits of Saints
Mosaic portraits **(above)** of biblical saints, laid out in rows of *kokoshniki* gables (tiered decorative arches), adorn the exterior of the church.

4 Window Frames
The window frames are carved out of marble transported from Estonia and cast in the form of traditional decorative patterns.

2 Steeple
The main steeple of the church is 81 m (265 ft) high. Steeples were banned in Russia in the 17th century by Metropolitan Nikon, who felt they were too similar to Western churches.

5 Mosaic Tympanum
The church's exterior **(below)** is made up of panels depicting scenes from the New Testament. During the Siege *(see p38)*, starving citizens gathered to pray under the Tympanum, finding solace in its depiction of Christ on his throne.

6 Alexander II Plaques
The perimeter of the lower wall has 20 dark-red plaques made of Norwegian granite, which illustrate key events of the 25-year reign of Alexander II (1855–81), including the emancipation of the serfs in 1861.

9 Icons
The church's interior walls and ceiling are covered in intricately detailed Old Russian mosaic icons **(left)** depicting a vast array of biblical figures and scenes.

A CHURCH IN HONOUR OF THE TSAR

The Church on Spilled Blood has never been used for weddings, funerals or any other church service. It was to be entirely dedicated to the memory of Alexander II, though some sermon readings did take place before the Revolution.

10 Bell Tower Coat of Arms
The 144 mosaics on the Bell Tower Coat of Arms **(below)** represent Russia's provinces, towns and regions at the time of the assassination.

NEED TO KNOW

MAP N2
■ Konyushennaya ploshchad ■ 315 1636
■ www.eng.cathedral.ru/ spasa_na_krovi

Open 10:30am–6pm (May–Sep: until 10 pm); closed Wed

Adm: P250 (P400 May–Sep: 6–10pm)

■ The façade of the church is undergoing a major restoration, which is planned to last until 2025, but the church is open to visitors.

■ After visiting the church, if the weather is good, head off to the Mikhaylovskiy Garden for a picnic lunch.

7 Alexander II's Shrine
Decorated with images of the tsar's patron saint, the shrine marks the exact spot where Alexander II was slain. Designed by Alfred Parland and completed in 1907, it was restored in the 1990s.

8 Restoration Exhibition
This is a fascinating exhibition depicting the state of the church prior to its restoration in the mid-1990s. Look out for the section of Alexander II's shrine that has been left in its previous condition to demonstrate the scale of the restorative work carried out on the detailed mosaics.

TOP 10 ★ Mariinskiy Theatre

The Mariinskiy Theatre has long been one of the world's most respected venues for opera and ballet. It has seen premieres by such greats as Tchaikovsky and Prokofiev, while the dance school produced Nureyev and Nijinsky. When it first opened to the public in 1860, the Mariinskiy boasted the largest stage in the world. A second stage, located just behind the original theatre, opened in 2013 and has some of the world's best acoustics. The original theatre is a St Petersburg institution, and a visit here is a highlight.

1 Royal Box
The Royal Box **(above)**, with its imperial eagles, lustrous curtains and sparkling chandeliers, is a vivid reminder of Imperial Russia. Tsars watched performances from here.

2 Stage Curtain
Designed by Aleksandr Golovin in 1914, during Russian ballet's golden age, the luxuriant stage curtain has revealed, then concealed, countless world-famous ballet dancers.

3 Programme
A programme of the event will make for a beautiful souvenir. Available in both English and Russian, the programmes are sold in the foyer and also at the ticket desk.

4 Performances
A performance at the Mariinskiy Theatre **(left)** is one that will stay with you for a long time. Not-to-be-missed productions include Tchaikovsky's *Eugene Onegin* and Mussorgsky's *Boris Godunov*. Also look out for opera stars Anna Netrebko, Olga Borodina and Vladimir Galouzine.

6 Façade

The façade of this Neo-Renaissance building **(above)** was remodelled in 1883–6 by Viktor Schröter, who added most of the ornamental detail.

7 Theatre Square

Once known as Carousel Square, Theatre Square and the surrounding canal-lined streets have long been home to the city's artistic community.

9 Ceiling

Don't forget to take a look at the Mariinskiy's intricate ceiling. Dating from 1856 and designed by Italian artist Enrico Franchioli, it depicts dancing girls and cupids.

8 Mariinsky II

This modernist structure (2013) dwarfs the original theatre building. It took a decade to build at a cost of £450 million, ten times the original budget.

5 Audiences

A fine place for people-spotting, those with an interest in the Russian government and pop culture may be lucky enough to spot celebrities from the worlds of politics and showbiz.

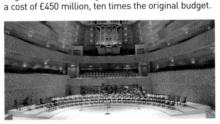

NEED TO KNOW

MAP B5 ▪ Teatralnaya ploschad 1 ▪ 326 4141 ▪ www.mariinsky.ru

Performances usually begin at 11:30am (matinee) or 7pm.

Tickets are more expensive for tourists than Russians and can cost anything from ₽500 to ₽5,000.

▪ Russians tend to dress up when attending the ballet or the opera. While a suit and tie or ballroom dress are not strictly necessary, guests should make an effort to fit in.

▪ After a show, Sadko (see p83) or Irish bar Shamrock (see p84) are good places to discuss the evening's performance over dinner.

10 Mariinskiy Concert Hall

Built on the site of the former Set Workshops, which were destroyed by fire in 2003, this stunning concert hall **(above)** was designed by Xavier Fabre in conjunction with Japanese acoustics master Yasuhisa Toyota. It hosts orchestras from all over the world.

TOP 10 ★ Russian Museum

While the Hermitage is home to art collected from all over the world, the Russian Museum is an exclusively Russian affair, its exhibits ranging from priceless 12th-century icons to the avant-garde paintings of Kandinsky and Malevich. Opened to the public for the first time in 1898, the museum was nationalized after the 1917 Revolution and its collection swelled by works confiscated from palaces and churches. From the 1930s until Gorbachev's restructuring, it exhibited mainly Socialist Realism art. The museum is housed in the 19th-century Mikhaylovskiy Palace, one of the finest Neo-Classical creations of Carlo Rossi, the Italian architect also responsible for Palace Square.

5 Perfected Portrait of Ivan Kliun
A distorted portrait by leading avant-garde painter Kazmir Malevich (1878–1935), which shows his obsession with simple geometric shapes.

6 Portrait of the Poetess Anna Akhmatova
Anna Akhmatova's (see p47) portrait, by Russian Cubist painter Nathan Altman (1889–1970), was completed in 1914, when Akhmatova was 25.

1 The Last Day of Pompeii
One of the first Russian paintings to attract attention abroad, Karl Bryullov's (1799–1852) magnificent creation **(above)** was the result of his visit to Pompeii immediately after an eruption of Mount Vesuvius in 1828.

2 Wrestlers
Natalia Goncharova (1881–1962), who had links to the Pushkin family (see p46), was deeply inspired by the primitivism of Russian folk art. *Wrestlers* (1908–09) is an example of her welding of Cubism and pre-revolutionary Russian avant-garde.

4 Pine Grove
Ivan Shishkin (1832–98), a contemporary of the Wanderers (see p90), was renowned for his soothing forest landscapes. The serene *Pine Grove* is a classic example of his desire to depict the beauty of nature in its pure, unadorned state.

7 Old Russian Decorative and Applied Art
This section of the museum has a collection of porcelain, furniture, glass and fascinating artifacts **(below)** that has been built up since 1895.

3 The Zaporozhye Cossacks Writing a Mocking Letter to the Turkish Sultan
Ilya Repin's colossal piece is based on the Ukrainian Cossacks' fight with Turkey in the 17th century.

8 Knight at the Crossroads

Russia's uncertain future at the *fin de siècle* is symbolized in Viktor Vasnetsov's (1848–1926) brooding and mournful knight **(above)**, a hyper-realistic painting remarkable for its imaginative use of colour.

9 Living Head

Despite having his work suppressed by the Soviets, Pavel Filonov (1883–1941) refused to sell any of his heavily detailed paintings, such as *Living Head*, to foreign collectors. A contemporary and close friend of the writer Daniil Kharms (*see p46*), Filonov perished during the siege of the city (*see p38*).

10 Descent into Hell Icon

Created some time in the 15th century, this icon, which survived the anti-religion purges after the 1917 Revolution, has been attributed to the Pskov school of icon painters.

Portrait of the Poetess Anna Akhmatova
6

Living Head
9

Knight at the Crossroads
8

Wrestlers
2

Perfected Portrait of Ivan Kliun
5

1 The Last Day of Pompeii

Russian Museum Floorplan

Old Russian Decorative and Applied Art
7

4 Pine Grove

Key to Floorplan
First floor
Ground floor

The Zaporozhye Cossacks Writing a Mocking Letter to the Turkish Sultan
3

Descent into Hell Icon 10

NEED TO KNOW

MAP N3 ■ Inzhenernaya ulitsa 4 ■ 595 4248; 314 6424 ■ www.rusmuseum.ru

Open 10am–8pm Mon (to 6pm Wed & Fri–Sun), 1–9pm Thu; closed Tue

Adm adults ₽450; children under-16s free

It is worth hiring an audio guide to accompany you on your visit to the museum. These are available in English and can be hired at the ticket office.

■ After visiting the museum, try some real Russian pancakes (*blini*) in the restaurant/café on the ground floor.

Museum Guide
The museum's exhibits are arranged chronologically, starting with the icons on the first floor. The exhibition then descends to the ground floor of the main building and Rossi Wing, and then back up to the first floor of the Benois Wing. Exhibitions are changed regularly.

Peter and Paul Fortress

First built in wood, and later in stone, the Peter and Paul Fortress dates from the founding of St Petersburg in 1703. During its construction, hundreds of serfs and Swedish prisoners of war perished in the murderous swamps that surrounded it. Containing a magnificent cathedral, dark, damp cells, a popular beach and fine examples of Baroque architecture, it is a contradictory wonder that at times exhilarates and, at times, chills the bones.

1 The Mint
Established in the early 18th century by Peter the Great, the mint **(above)** remains in use today, one of only two places in Russia (the other being in Moscow) where coins, along with medals and badges, are minted.

2 St Peter's Gate
The gate (1718) depicts St Peter's banishment of the winged mystic, Simon Magus. This Baroque construction with scrolled wings **(above)** allegorizes Peter the Great's victory at the Battle of Poltava in 1709.

3 Cathedral of SS Peter and Paul
This Baroque cathedral **(right)** was an attempt by Peter the Great to reject traditional Russian church architecture. The remains of tsars from the Romanov dynasty are inside.

4 Neva Gate
Built in 1784–7, the Neva Gate was referred to as "Death Gate" during the years it was used to transport prisoners to their execution in the neighbouring Schlusselburg Fortress. The archway contains plaques that commemorate record flood levels.

5 Trubetskoy Bastion
The dark cells of the Trubetskoy Bastion served as a prison. The first prisoner here was Aleksey, who was accused of plotting treason by his father, Peter the Great, and executed in 1718.

6 Engineer's House
This building (1749) was once used as living quarters for the engineers of the city's garrison. It now houses exhibitions dedicated to St Petersburg's pre-revolutionary days.

A FORTRESS AGAINST THE SWEDES

The Peter and Paul Fortress was originally intended to provide protection for the new city against possible incursions and attacks by the Swedish navy. However, the Swedes were defeated even before the finishing touches had been put to the fortress. Thus stripped of its original intended function, it was turned over to the local garrison. It also served as a prison for political dissenters.

7 The Beach
During summer, the beach **(above)** is full of sunbathers. In winter, it becomes the exclusive haunt of "The Walruses", a group of St Petersburg citizens who break through the thick ice to dip into the freezing waters beneath.

8 Statue of Peter the Great
Mikhail Chemiakin's statue **(right)** caused great controversy upon its unveiling in 1991. Intended to depict Peter the Great's "alter-ego", the statue portrays the founder of St Petersburg with a very tiny head and spindly fingers.

9 Commandant's House
A reminder of more unpleasant aspects of the fortress's history, this early 18th-century structure is where political prisoners were interrogated during the years of tsarist rule.

10 The Grand Ducal Burial Vault
The vault (1908) was constructed to replace the already overflowing cathedral as the final resting place of the tsars.

NEED TO KNOW

MAP C2 ▪ Petropavlovskaya krepost ▪ 230 6431
▪ www.spbmuseum.ru

Grounds: open 6am–10pm

Fortress: open 9:30am–9pm

Cathedral: open 10am–7pm Mon–Fri (to 5:45pm Sat),

11am–7pm Sun; adm adults ₽450; children ₽250; seniors ₽200; ticket includes entrance to the cathedral and a guided tour.

▪ Set aside an entire morning or afternoon for a visit to the fortress. The riverside beach is perfect for sunbathing.

▪ There are many cafés within the grounds of the fortress. During summer, another option is to take a picnic to the beach.

Following pages St Isaac's Cathedral in winter

TOP 10 ★ St Isaac's Cathedral

The smaller church of the same name commissioned by Peter the Great was destroyed in floods soon after its construction in 1710. The larger, present-day St Isaac's opened in 1858 and was designed by French architect Auguste de Montferrand. The cathedral weighs 300,000 tonnes and contains 400 kilograms of gold in its interior decoration. The engineering operation needed to erect it was, at the time, of an almost unprecedented scale. Used as a museum of atheism during the Soviet years, the cathedral is the second largest in Russia.

1 Internal Walls
The interiors of the cathedral **(above)** are adorned with 14 different types of coloured marble and over 40 types of semi-precious stones.

2 St Catherine's Chapel
This chapel is remarkable for its "Resurrection" (1850–54) – a stunning hybrid of Baroque and Classical styles. Sculpted by the artist Nikolay Pimenov, it is the crowning point of the exquisite white marble iconostasis.

3 Ceiling Painting
"The Virgin in Majesty" (1847), the fresco that adorns the inside of the cathedral's cupola **(right)**, was created by Karl Bryullov and covers 816 sq m (8,780 sq ft).

4 The Dome
Accessed via a colonnaded walkway, St Isaac's gilded viewing dome **(right)** is decorated with angels created by sculptor Josef Hermann. The dome offers breathtaking views across the city.

5 Statues of the Apostles
Statues of the apostles stand guard atop the cathedral, with Mark with a lion, Matthew with an angel, John with an eagle and Luke with a calf at the four compass points.

6 South Doors
The south portico has three great double-shuttered doors made of cast bronze over oak. They are decorated with biblical scenes.

8 Red Granite Columns

The 48 columns **(left)** in the cathedral were specially imported from Finland at tremendous cost and effort.

9 Iconostasis

Three rows of icons surround the royal doors, above which is Pyotr Klodt's gilded "Christ in Majesty".

HUMAN SUFFERING

The construction of St Isaac's Cathedral over 40 years was accompanied by much suffering and sacrifice of human life. Hundreds of serfs lost their lives, crushed to death by falling chunks of marble. At least 60 people were killed by inhaling the mercury fumes used in the dome's elaborate gilding process.

10 Angels with Torch

The reverent angels holding up the gas torches that crown the four corners of the cathedral **(below)** were created by Ivan Vitali, who was responsible for many of the other figures that adorn the cathedral.

7 Traces of Nazi Bombardment

St Isaac's was hit by artillery bombardment during the World War II siege *(see p38)*. Traces of this can be found on the left-hand side of the cathedral's steps as a reminder of the war years.

NEED TO KNOW

MAP K4 ■ Isaakievskaya ploshchad ■ 315 9732 ■ www.eng.cathedral.ru/ isakievskii_sobor

Open May–Sep: 10am– 10:30pm Thu–Tue; Oct–Apr: 10:30am–6pm Thu–Tue; closed third Wed of month

Colonnaded Walkway: open May–Oct: 10am– 10:30pm daily (1 Jun–20 Aug: to 4:30am); Nov–Apr: 10:30am–6pm Thu–Tue; closed Wed; adm: adults ₽250; children ₽50

■ St Isaac's is most impressive around dusk

during the winter, when it dominates the snowy skyline like some giant sentinel standing guard in the vastness of St Isaac's Square.

■ A popular café, Idiot *(see p76)*, is close by and does great set lunches.

TOP10 ⭐ Peterhof

An extravagant collection of palaces, fountains and gardens, Peterhof lies on the shore of the Gulf of Finland. Having originally come across the site in 1705, Peter the Great commissioned the building of a palace here in 1714. He intended the estate to rival that of Versailles in France. The Great Palace (1714–21), originally designed by Jean Baptiste Le Blond, was transformed during the reign of Elizabeth by Bartolomeo Rastrelli, architect of the Winter Palace, who added its distinctive Baroque element.

1 The Grand Cascade
Comprising 37 gilded bronze sculptures, 64 fountains and 142 water jets, the Grand Cascade **(above)** descends from the terraces of the Great Palace, through the estate, and finally out into the gulf.

2 The Throne Room
This opulent room, initially created in Baroque style in 1753 and redesigned by Yuriy Velten in 1770, contains portraits of Russia's imperial family.

3 The Imperial Suite
Located in the palace's east wing, the suite contains Peter's Oak Study – a rare example of Le Blond's original design. The oak panels date from 1716–21.

4 Cottage Palace
More imposing than its name suggests, this Neo-Gothic house (1826–9), set in the gardens of Alexandria Park, was built for Nicholas I and his wife, who had bourgeois tastes and wanted a domestic environment.

5 The Main Staircase
With its allegorical sculpture of Elizabeth in the guise of Spring, Rastrelli's creation **(below)** is a stately sight.

8 Marly Palace

This charming Baroque mansion **(left)** was built as an intimate retreat for the tsar and his guests, and is set in a formal garden with sculptures, fountains and Niccolo Michetti's Golden Hill Cascade. A few of the rooms are open to the public.

NAZI OCCUPATION

Peterhof was occupied for three years during World War II by Nazi soldiers laying siege to the city. They burnt the Great Palace and extensively damaged several of the structures. The estate was gradually restored after the war.

9 Monplaisir

Monplaisir ("my pleasure" in French), with its beautiful gardens and flowerbeds **(above)**, was Peter's favourite palace. He often held parties here, in which guests took part in a punishing regime of drinking. The interiors, not as lavish as the Great Palace, are still impressive.

10 The Neptune Fountain

The Neptune Fountain's Baroque sculpture, the central feature of the Upper Gardens, was originally erected in Nuremberg, Germany, in 1658. It was sold to Paul II in 1782 by local authorities as a lack of water in the town had rendered it unusable.

6 The Hermitage

This pavilion (1721–5), once used as a private dining venue by the tsar and his friends, stands aloof on the shores of the gulf. To highlight the need for solitude, the building is surrounded by a moat.

7 The Pyramid Fountain

The fountain (1721) is formed by 550 jets rising in seven tiers. Commemorating the Russian victory over Sweden in 1709, it was badly damaged by Nazi bombs during World War II.

NEED TO KNOW

MAP G1 ■ Peterhof, 30 km (19 miles) W of St Petersburg ■ 450 5287 ■ www.peterhof museum.ru

Great Palace:
open 10:30am–6pm Tue–Sun; closed last Tue of month; adm: adults ₽1,000, children under-16s free (with valid ID proof)

Parks: open 9am–8pm Mon–Fri & Sun (to 9pm Sat); adm: adults ₽700, children under-16s free

Fountains: open mid-May–Oct: 11am–6pm daily (to 8:50pm Sat & to 7pm Sun)

■ An exciting way to travel to or from Peterhof is by hydrofoil. Boats depart from the Gulf of Finland and leave St Petersburg from Dvortsovaya nab, near the Winter Palace *(see p14)*. Boats run early Jun–early Oct every hour from 9:30am to 6pm daily. The journey takes less than an hour.

■ Restaurants and cafés are scattered around the estate.

⭐ Tsarskoe Selo

These magnificent palaces and gardens were established as a country retreat by Catherine I, wife of Peter the Great, but it was Tsarina Elizabeth who commissioned the lavish Catherine Palace. The palace was initially created by Rastrelli, but later redesigned by Scottish architect Charles Cameron, at the request of Catherine the Great. The 18th-century landscaped gardens were the first of their kind in Russia. Tsarskoe Selo suffered extensive damage in World War II and restoration work continues to this day.

1 Amber Room
Created in Prussia, the room's amber panels were gifted to Peter the Great in 1716. Looted by Nazi troops during World War II, it took 24 years, until 2003, to recreate the room **(above)** using historical photographs.

2 The Great Hall
This magnificent room **(below)**, located in the Catherine Palace, features mirrors, ornate carvings and a huge ceiling painting, *The Triumph of Russia* (c.1755), created by Giuseppe Valeriani.

3 Green Dining Room
The pistachio-coloured walls of the room, designed by Charles Cameron, are decorated with stucco figures produced by the Russian Neo-Classical sculptor Ivan Martos.

4 The Great Staircase
The central staircase at Catherine Palace was designed by Ippolito Monighetti, and built in 1860. The landing walls are adorned with 18th- and 19th-century Oriental vases and dishes.

5 Formal Gardens
These lovely gardens **(above)** are laid out symmetrically, and include finely trimmed trees and hedges, as well as geometrically planned flowerbeds complemented by strategically placed marble statues.

9 The Cameron Gallery

This Neo-Classical section **(left)** of the Catherine Palace features busts of philosophers and thinkers. It was a favourite with Catherine, especially during her later years.

6 The Blue Drawing Room

Notable for its unusual wallpaper – blue floral motifs painted on silk – this room contains a portrait of Peter the Great by Ivan Nitkin, dating from 1720.

7 Small Enfilade

A long, captivating suite of halls, parlours and reception rooms, the Small Enfilade boasts a wide collection of period furniture. It also contains some fine examples of Oriental rugs.

10 The Grotto

Construction of Rastrelli's Grotto **(above)** began in 1749, but the interior, comprising over 250,000 shells, was not finished for 25 years.

8 The Cavalier's Dining Room

Elizabeth's gentlemen-in-waiting dined here. The table is permanently laid in this refined gold and white room, designed by Rastrelli.

AHEAD OF ITS TIME

This town, originally called Tsarskoe Selo, was renamed in 1937 in honour of Russia's national poet Pushkin *(see p46),* who attended school here in 1811–17. Founded in the 19th century, the town boasted the first citywide electrical system in Europe, as well as advanced sewage and water systems. It was also the home of the first radio station (1916) in Russia.

NEED TO KNOW

MAP H2 ■ 25 km (16 miles) W of St Petersburg ■ 466 6669; 465 2024

Palace: open Oct–Apr: 10am– 5pm; May & Sep: noon–6pm (Jun–Aug: to 7pm); closed Tue, Oct–Apr: last Mon of month; adm: adults ₽1000; students ₽350; under-16s free

Park: open Sep–Apr: 7am–9pm (May–Jun: to 11pm & Jul–Aug: to 10pm); adm: Oct–late Apr: free; rest of the year: adults ₽150; students ₽80; under-16s free

■ Take a train from Vitebskiy station to Detskoe Selo, then bus 371 or 382. Or from Moskovskaya ploshchad (next to the metro station), take minibuses K-286, K-287, K-342, K-347 or K-545, or bus 187.

■ Avoid Tsarskoe Selo on national holidays as it can get rather crowded.

■ The Imperial Palace Restaurant at the Catherine Palace is a convenient place for a snack or a meal.

🔟 ⭐ Pavlovsk

Pavlovsk, an 18th-century park and palace ensemble, is notable for its atmospheric landscaped grounds, containing temples, pavilions and stone bridges. Catherine the Great gave the estate to her son, the future Paul I, in 1777 and Pavlovsk (from "Pavel" or Paul) was named in his honour. Architect Charles Cameron was commissioned to begin work on it in 1780, and Paul I's wife, Maria Fyodorovna, was the driving force behind the development of the palace's exhaustive collections. Maria, being infatuated with both Pavlovsk and Europe, travelled with Paul throughout the continent, bringing back many sculptures, paintings and silk sets.

1 Pavlovsk Palace

This modest palace (1782–6) **(centre)** consists of a series of remarkably well-preserved rooms and halls that afford the visitor a revealing glimpse into the lifestyle of Russia's pre-revolutionary nobility.

2 The Rose Pavilion

Maria Fyodorovna often entertained guests in this cottage designed around the theme of the rose **(above)**. Alexander I's victory over Napoleon was celebrated here too.

4 Visconti Bridge

The most famous bridge in the park was designed by Andrey Voronikhin in 1807. Its arch stretches lazily over the river, reflected in the water to form a graceful oval.

5 The Muses

The nine Muses (1780–98), which were based on statues gracing the museums of Italy's Rome and Florence, were created in the workshops of the Russian Academy.

3 Pil Tower and Bridge

Built by Vincenzo Brenna in 1795, this tower with a conical straw roof **(right)** at one time contained a spiral staircase, library and opulent lounge. The nearby bridge was added later in 1808.

6 The Apollo Colonnade

This graceful colonnade **(above)** encircles a copy of the Apollo Belvedere. Following a storm in 1817, an iron Apollo replaced the bronze original.

8 Cameron's Dairy

Important visitors to the estate were invited to this working dairy, a small building with a thatched roof, to sample simple peasant fare.

7 Cold Baths

This austere pavilion was constructed by Cameron in 1799 as a summer swimming pool. It had an elegant vestibule, paintings, furniture and rich wall upholstery.

9 Paul's Mausoleum

Despite the name, and construction in the form of an ancient Roman temple, it never held Paul I's remains. It bears the inscription "To my beneficent consort".

A SCOTTISH ARCHITECT IN RUSSIA

Having read Charles Cameron's book about Roman public baths, Catherine the Great invited the architect to Russia to work on the reconstruction of her summer palace at Tsarskoe Selo *(see pp32–3)*. Pleased with his work, she "lent" him to her son, then Grand Duke Paul, to work on the Pavlovsk estate.

10 Temple of Friendship

This Doric temple (1780) **(below)**, dedicated to Catherine the Great, is the earliest example of Greek forms in Russia.

NEED TO KNOW

MAP H2 ■ 30 km (19 miles) S of St Petersburg ■ 452 1536 ■ www.pavlovsk museum.ru

Palace: open 10am–6pm daily; closed 1st Mon of month; palace & park adm adults ₽500, children ₽200

(last adm 45 min before closing); ticket office closes at 5pm

Park: open 6am–11pm daily; adm adults ₽100, children ₽50 (free adm 6–9am & 7–11pm)

■ Take the train from **Vitebskiy** or **Kupchino**

stations, then take bus 370, 383, 493, K-286 or K-299.

■ One of the pleasures of Pavlovsk is strolling through its romantic grounds, so be sure to pay a visit when the weather is fine.

■ There are restaurants in the Great Hall of the Pavlovsk Palace.

The Top 10 of Everything

**Ballet dancers in the wings at the
Mariinskiy Theatre**

🔟 Moments in History

Painting depicting Bloody Sunday by Ivan Vladimirov

Founding of the City
St Petersburg was founded by Peter the Great in 1703 as Russia's "Window to Europe". Constructed on swampland, it was built by thousands of serfs, many of whom perished, their bones laying the city's foundations. It became the capital of Russia in 1712, and remained so until 1918.

2 "Bloody Sunday"
On 9 January 1905, peaceful demonstrators carrying a petition to Nicholas II were gunned down by the army as they marched towards the Winter Palace. Around 1,000 demonstrators perished. The aftermath of the horrifying event led to the 1905 Revolution.

3 1917 Revolution
Following a series of strikes in 1917, the tsar was forced to abdicate, and a provisional government assumed power. This was the signal for exiled revolutionaries, led by Vladimir Lenin, to return to Russia, where they overthrew the fledgling government in October, heralding the start of more than 70 years of Soviet rule.

4 World War II Siege
The 900-day Siege of Leningrad, which began in 1941 when Nazi forces encircled the city, plunged its three million inhabitants into a living hell. By the time the siege was finally broken in 1944, around two million people had lost their lives to starvation and bitterly cold winters.

5 1991 Coup
The military coup occurred when hardliners opposed to President Gorbachev's reforms seized power. Supporters of Gorbachev's policies gathered in Palace Square (see p14) to protest events. The coup was eventually defeated.

Protesters in Palace Square in 1991

6 The City's Name Changes

Founded as St Petersburg, the city's name was changed to the more Russian sounding Petrograd in 1914, then to Leningrad in 1924, after the death of Vladimir Lenin. Its original name was restored following the collapse of the USSR in 1991.

7 "Criminal" 1990s

Immediately after the era of *perestroika*, a criminal class sprung up, willing and able to do anything to build up fortunes. During this period, St Petersburg earned the reputation as the "Crime Capital of Russia".

8 Reburial of Nicholas II

After the 1917 Revolution, Nicholas II and his family were executed in Yekaterinburg. In 1998, their remains were reburied in the Cathedral of SS Peter and Paul (see pp26–7).

Reburial of Nicholas II and his family

9 300th Anniversary

The year 2003 heralded St Petersburg's 300th anniversary and saw a long-needed renovation of the city. The celebrations were attended by the heads of government from more than 45 countries and lasted for over ten days.

10 Election of Vladimir Putin

A St Petersburg native, Putin came into power as Acting President on New Year's Eve, 1999. He oversaw years of economic growth in his first presidential term, but his current term has seen economic difficulties, with falling oil prices and the imposition of Western sanctions following the annexation of Crimea in 2014.

TOP 10 ST PETERSBURG POLITICAL FIGURES

Portrait of Lenin by Isaak Brodksy

1 Peter the Great
The driving force behind the city, Peter the Great ruled Russia from 1682 to 1725.

2 Nicholas II
The last tsar of Russia was killed by the Bolsheviks after the 1917 Revolution.

3 Rasputin
A peasant mystic whose scandalous lifestyle helped discredit Nicholas II's rule (see p80).

4 Mikhail Bakunin
A revolutionary involved in insurrections all over Europe, generally considered the "father of modern anarchism".

5 Lenin
Leader of the 1917 Revolution and the first head of the Soviet Union, Lenin changed Russia forever.

6 Sergey Kirov
A Soviet revolutionary whose assassination marked the beginning of a series of purges in the 1930s.

7 Anatoly Sobchak
St Petersburg's first democratically elected mayor took office in 1991 and was instrumental in restoring the original name of the city.

8 Galina Starovoitova
Known for her democratic principles, this politician was assassinated in 1998.

9 Valentina Matvienko
The governor of the city from 2003 to 2011, Matvienko rose to national office as Chairman of the Federation Council.

10 Vladimir Putin
Elected President of the Russian Federation in 2000, Putin spent 2008–12 as prime minister before regaining the presidency once more in 2012.

TOP10 Bridges and Waterways

The stunning Lion Bridge, a famous St Petersburg landmark

1 Lion Bridge

The two pairs of proud lions on Lion Bridge (Lviny Most), a Pavel Sokolov creation, date from 1825–6 *(see p79)*. One of the city's earliest pedestrian suspension bridges, it is suspended by chains emerging from the mouths of the cast-iron lions.

2 Trinity Bridge
MAP M1

Opened in 1903 to commemorate the 200th anniversary of the founding of St Petersburg, Trinity Bridge (Troitskiy

Bronze statue on Anichkov Bridge

Most) is one of the most beautiful of the city's 800 bridges. It consists of ten arches and elegant Style-Moderne lampposts.

3 Anichkov Bridge
MAP P4

The three-span Anichkov Bridge (1839–41) is noteworthy for its evocative bronze statues of men taming wild horses by Russian sculptor Pyotr Klodt. The statues symbolize man's taming of the forces of Mother Nature. Viewed in an anti-clockwise direction, the wild horses seem to steadily become domesticated.

4 Lomonosov Bridge
MAP N5

Notable for its curious stone turrets, this bridge is named in honour of the Russian scientist Mikhail Lomonosov (1711–65). Built between 1785 and 1787, its granite towers housed the opening mechanism. When the bridge was rebuilt in 1912, the towers, having become a landmark, were left in place.

5 Bridge Passage
MAP N1

Linking the junction of the Griboedov Canal and the Moyka river, the Bridge Passage (Bolshoi Obukhovsky Most), built 1829–31, is a cleverly constructed piece of architecture. Consisting of the Malo-Konyushenny and Theatre bridges. It has been designed to give the impression of a single bridge, the Bridge Passage contains beautiful metal railings and lampposts.

6 Bank Bridge
MAP M4

Dating from 1825–6, the pleasant Bankovsky pedestrian bridge is less than 2 m (7 ft) wide. It is famous throughout Russia for its four gold-winged griffins, created by Russian sculptor Pavel Sokolov. Seated in eternal contemplation of the waters below, they also serve to hold up the bridge's cables.

7 Griboedov Canal
MAP K6–M2

This canal, stretching 5 km (3 miles) through the very centre of the city, is crossed by 21 bridges. It was constructed in 1739 to move cargo from Sennaya ploshchad, and named after the Russian playwright and diplomat, Alexander Griboedov.

Striking views at Griboedov Canal

8 Egyptian Bridge
MAP B6

The splendid Egipetskiy Most dates from 1955. The current structure replaced the 19th-century original, which collapsed into the Fontanka in 1905, when a large cavalry squadron was passing by. The magnificent sphinxes that adorn the bridge were salvaged from the original bridge, as were the bank supports.

Railing of Blagoveshchenskiy Bridge

9 Blagoveshchenskiy Bridge

This elegant bridge *(see p89)*, which has also been known as the Nicholas Bridge and the Lieutenant Shmidt Bridge since its construction in 1850, was the first permanent crossing over the Neva river. The bridge retains its original, intricate cast-iron seahorse and trident railings, designed by Aleksandr Bryullov. Offering great views across the Admiralty and Universitet embankments, this is one of the city's most historic bridges, and a local landmark.

10 Winter Canal
MAP C3

The narrowest waterway in the city, the Winter Canal (Zimnyaya kanavka) is, nonetheless, one of its most picturesque. Constructed in 1718–20, this stretch of water is crossed by three bridges, and by the Hermitage's Theatre Foyer. Namechecked in Pushkin's *(see p46)* "Queen of Spades", the Winter Canal, particularly beautiful on a freezing winter's day, is a favourite for romantic trysts.

TOP 10 Soviet Landmarks

4 Lenin's Train
Finland Station (see p101) was opened in the mid-1960s, and contains Locomotive 293, the train on which Lenin rode when returning from exile to Russia to launch the 1917 Revolution that would bring him to power. Once a requisite sight for any Soviet visitor, this train, exhibited in a glass case on platform 5, attracts far less attention these days.

1 Revolution Square
Revolution Square was the name given by the Soviets to the site of one of the most brutal scenes of "Bloody Sunday" (see p38). Now known as Trinity Square, it is a pleasant leafy space (see p96).

2 Statue of Lenin in Ploshchad Lenina
MAP E2
This statue of Lenin, erected in 1926, portrays him delivering a fiery speech to cheering crowds following his return from exile in 1917.

3 Museum of Russian Political History
Lenin gave one of his many inspiring speeches from a balcony at this mansion (see p97), which is named after ballerina Matilda Kshesinskaya. Now a museum, it contains Lenin's office, restored to its Soviet-era state. Memorabilia from the period of revolutionary struggle are housed upstairs.

Museum of Russian Political History

5 Siege Plaque
This plaque was put up during the darkest days of the Siege of Leningrad (see p38) to warn citizens that the side of the road on which it sat was the most dangerous during an artillery attack. It is a stark reminder of the horrors of World War II, when millions of the city's citizens starved to death.

Façade of the Smolnyy Institute

6 Smolnyy Institute
MAP G3 ■ Ploshchad Proletarskoy Diktatury 3 ■ 576 7461 ■ Open by appointment only
This Neo-Classical building was at one time a school for young noblewomen, but during the days following the 1917 Revolution, it was the seat of government. Lenin ruled from here until March 1918, when the Soviets moved the capital to Moscow.

Avtovo station, one of the city's attractive metro stations

7 Cruiser Aurora

The cruiser *Aurora (see p95)* is famed as the ship that fired a blank shot to signal the storming of the Winter Palace, which then began the 1917 Revolution. Today it is open to the public, and the famous gun, along with the crew's quarters, can be viewed.

8 Kirov Museum

This museum *(see p95)* is located in the one-time flat of Sergey Kirov, a Stalin-era politician. Charismatic Kirov reportedly enjoyed grassroots popularity, leading Stalin to fear him as a rival. Most historians believe that Stalin arranged Kirov's assassination, and then used it as an excuse to launch a series of purges to punish the "guilty".

9 The Metro

Designed as monuments to the working class, the city's pre-*perestroika* metro stations *(see pp48–9)* are socialist palaces, complete with chandeliers, marble columns, mosaics and murals. It is as if the USSR never ceased to exist and the Cold War never ended – the stations' walls still bear hammers and sickles, and slogans extolling the achievements of the Soviet system.

10 Monument to the Heroic Defenders of Leningrad

Erected in 1975 to mark the 30th anniversary of the end of World War II, the Monument to the Heroic Defenders of Leningrad *(see p103)* commemorates the victims of the siege – it features sculptures of grieving mothers and defiant Soviet soldiers. A Memorial Hall at the complex has exhibits about life during the siege.

Monument to the Heroic Defenders of Leningrad

🔟 Museums

Throne room at the Hermitage

1 The Hermitage

A treasure trove, an architectural wonder, a symbol of the city's stubborn resistance during World War II – the Hermitage (see pp14–17) is all this and more. The vast collection features works by Michelangelo, Picasso and Rubens.

2 Kunstkammer

The Kunstkammer was the city's first museum, built between 1718 and 1734 to house Peter the Great's collection of anatomical curiosities (see p89). The first exhibition included live dwarves, giants and two-headed animals. Peter instructed the museum to offer free salo (pig fat) and vodka to boost attendance. Some of the original exhibits are still on display.

3 Russian Museum

Containing a wide range of works and styles, from the ground-breaking avant-garde art of Kazimir Malevich to the massive canvases of Karl Bryullov, this museum boasts one of the world's best collections of Russian art (see pp22–3).

4 Central Naval Museum

Founded in 1805 and moved to its current location in 2013, this is one of Russia's oldest museums (see p80). With over 700,000 maritime exhibits, it covers hundreds of years of naval history. Highlights of the collection include its intricate, 18th-century model ships, and the miniaturized warship Peter the Great learned to sail as a child.

Painting at the Central Naval Museum

5 Artillery Museum

Military enthusiasts will find a visit to this museum (see p96), housed in the outer fortifications of the Peter and Paul Fortress (see pp24–5), particularly rewarding. Used at one time as an arsenal,

Exterior of the Artillery Museum

the museum contains more than 600 exhibits, ranging from tanks and rocket launchers to an armoured car that Lenin rode in during the heady days of the 1917 Revolution.

6 Museum of Soviet Arcade Machines

This retro museum (see p74) has rapidly become one of the city's most popular attractions. It is packed with Soviet-era arcade games dating from the 1970s and 1980s, which visitors can play with old 15 *kopek* coins. Fun for both children and nostalgic adults, there's also an old *kvas* dispensing machine.

7 Stieglitz Museum

Taking its name from Baron Aleksandr Stieglitz, a wealthy industrialist who started an art collection to aid the education of local students in 1876, the museum (see p101) contains exhaustive displays of decorative arts, glassware and ceramics. The stunning, medieval-style Terem Room is a real highlight.

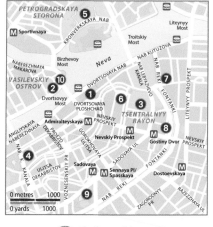

Stieglitz Museum

8 Fabergé Museum

Housed within the lavishly restored Shuvalov Palace, the centre-pieces of this fabulous exhibition (see p68) are nine of the 50 bejewelled Fabergé eggs that were presented as Easter gifts by the last two Russian tsars to their mothers and wives. The collection, amassed by Viktor Vekselberg, includes the first and last of the imperial eggs and the famous Coronation Egg, which contains a tiny replica of the Imperial coach. The museum also displays a wide range of other *objets d'art*.

9 Railway Museum

This museum (see p81) boasts comprehensive displays on the history of the Russian railway system from its inauguration in 1813. Exhibits include a model of a formidable-looking armoured train used to transport Bolshevik revolutionaries in 1917.

10 Zoological Museum

The Zoological Museum (see p91) has one of the world's best collections of mammoths, including a 44,000-year-old specimen dug up in Siberia in 1902. Dating from 1826, the museum contains over one and a half million specimens, including stuffed bears and giant crabs.

Exhibits in the Zoological Museum

🔟 Writers

Alexander Pushkin

1 Pushkin (1799–1837)
Alexander Pushkin's masterpiece is *Evgeniy Onegin* (1825–32), a novel set in verse form. He was the first writer to explore the rich potential of the Russian language as spoken by the common people. He was killed in a duel.

2 Gogol (1809–52)
Although born in the Ukraine, a huge amount of Nikolai Gogol's strikingly original work, such as *The Nose* (1835) and *The Overcoat* (1842), is set in St Petersburg.

3 Dostoevsky (1821–81)
The author of some of the world's most profound literature, such as *Crime and Punishment* (1866), Fyodor Dostoevsky spent much of his life in St Petersburg. It was here in 1849 that he was subjected to a mock execution for "revolutionary activities", the trauma of which influenced his future literary work.

Fyodor Dostoevsky

4 Mandelstam (1891–1938)
The author of symbolic, taut poetry, Osip Mandelstam composed in 1933 his infamous, untitled poem about Stalin, in which he wrote of the dictator's "cockroach whiskers" and his "fingers as fat as grubs". The poem, which ultimately led to his death, became known as the "16-line death sentence".

5 Kharms (1905–42)
Daniil Kharms wrote some of the most original Russian literature, which was suppressed by Stalin due to its downright oddness rather than any overt political message. The absurdist writer starved to death in the World War II siege of the city *(see p38)*.

Daniil Kharms

6 Bely (1880–1934)
Although born in Moscow, Andrey Bely reached the pinnacle of his career with his symbolist masterpiece, *Petersburg* (1913), a chaotic, prophetic novel that has been compared to the works of Irish writer James Joyce.

7 Nabokov (1899–1977)
Best known for *Lolita*, Vladimir Nabokov was born in St Petersburg in 1899 and grew up trilingual, fluent in Russian, English and French. His family moved to Europe in 1918 and he wrote many of his novels in English.

Joseph Brodsky

8 Brodsky (1940–96)

Joseph Brodsky, protégé of Akhmatova, won the Nobel Prize for Literature in 1987. He left the USSR in 1972 after his works were attacked by the authorities.

9 Akhmatova (1889–1966)

Branded a "half-harlot, half-nun" by Soviet authorities in 1946, the poet Anna Akhmatova wrote *Requiem* (1940), her tragic masterpiece about the terrifying Stalin years, which was banned in the USSR until 1989. Her first husband was killed by the Bolsheviks.

Anna Akhmatova

10 Blok (1880–1921)

Central to the "Silver Age" of Russian poetry, Alexander Blok developed complex poetic symbols. His controversial work, *The Twelve*, likens Bolshevik soldiers to Christ's Apostles.

TOP 10 FILMS SET IN ST PETERSBURG

1 October (1927)
Sergei Eisenstein's film, an epic depiction of the 1917 Revolution, is a silent black-and-white masterpiece.

2 The End of St Petersburg (1927)
Another film dedicated to the 1917 Revolution, Pudovkin's film forms part of the director's *Revolutionary Trilogy*.

3 The Irony of Fate (1975)
A romantic comedy that uses as its plot device the extreme similarity of Soviet housing.

4 The Burglar (1986)
A *perestroika* favourite, this film portrays the city's underground rock scene.

5 GoldenEye (1995)
British spy James Bond comes to St Petersburg to carry out a daring raid involving the Russian Mafia in this action-packed film.

6 Brother (1997)
A bleak yet humorous film that depicts the chaos of mid-1990s St Petersburg.

7 Russian Ark (2002)
The world's first unedited feature film, *Russian Ark* is a 90-minute wander through the Winter Palace *(see p14)*.

8 The Idiot (2003)
A highly successful and popular Russian TV adaptation of Dostoevsky's famous novel *The Idiot*.

9 The Stroll (2003)
Three young people wander around the city discussing life and love.

10 Garpastum (2003)
Love, war and football (*garpastum* means "ball game" in Latin) take equal billing in this impressive film by Alexsei German Jr, set in 1914.

A still from *October*

Metro Highlights

1 Ploshchad Vosstaniya Station

MAP E4

While the interior of the station is highly ornate, the distinguished exterior – a curious circular structure topped with a steeple – has a crumbling beauty. The station, part of the 1955 Line One construction, is dedicated to the 1917 Revolution. Today the building is the subject of ongoing restoration work and is, at times, obscured by scaffolding.

Ploshchad Vosstaniya station

2 Frunzenskaya Station

Named in honour of the Bolshevik leader Mikhail Frunze, Frunzenskaya metro station was opened in 1961 as part of St Petersburg's Line Two project. Its central feature is a large monument depicting Frunze with his revolutionary comrades. In comparison with many other stations in the city, Frunzenskaya has a relatively simple design, notable for its absence of ornate chandeliers and marble columns.

3 Kirovskiy Zavod Station

Kirovskiy Zavod station (1955), which means "Kirov Factory station", is named after a nearby factory. Although the station's elegant design, with its marble columns and wide platform, was intended to pay homage to the achievements of Soviet industry, the building resembles an ancient Greek temple.

4 Mezhdunarodnaya Station

This modern station opened in 2012. The name means "International" and is taken from the many local streets named after East European politicians. Its most noteworthy feature is an impressive mosaic of Atlas holding up the world.

5 Avtovo Station

The Avtovo station, like the vast majority of metro stations in Russia, was constructed during the Soviet period. It opened in 1955 and was intended to act as one of many "Palaces for the People". Complete with chandeliers and marble columns, this station reveals a fascinating part of the city's history. The station's

Ornate Avtovo Station

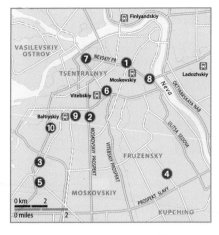

8 Ploshchad Alexandra Nevskogo Station
MAP G5

Ploshchad Alexandra Nevskogo is notable for the colourful mural immediately inside the entrance, which depicts Russia's defeat of Swedish invaders in the 13th century. Opened in 1985, this was St Petersburg's first station on the Pravoberezhnaya (right bank) Line.

9 Baltiskaya Station

Another Line One metro station dating from 1955, Baltiskaya station features a large image of Baltic socialist revolutionaries from Latvia, Estonia and Lithuania, hoisting the red flag of socialism aloft in victory. Its exterior is a massive Socialist Realism construction typical of the period.

Woman with Child mosaic is topped with the words "Peace to the World".

6 Pushkinskaya Station
MAP D5

Named after Pushkin, Russia's national poet *(see p46)*, this station is one of the most beautiful in St Petersburg. A statue of a pensive Pushkin is the centrepiece of the station, which is a masterpiece of architectural design. Pushkinskaya station was opened in 1956, later than the other stations on Line One, due to problems with tunneling.

Statue at Pushkinskaya station

10 Narvskaya Station

The sculpted figures in this station *(see p91)* are gazing at someone who is no longer there – it's Stalin (1878–1953), the dictator whose once ubiquitous image was removed from the USSR following Nikita Khrushchev's "secret" denouncement of Stalinism in 1956.

7 Admiralteyskaya Station
MAP L3

Opened in 2011, and built 86 m (282 ft) below ground to avoid damaging the nearby Hermitage, this station with marine decor is one of the world's deepest underground stations – Kiev's Arsenalna station is the deepest at 107 m (351 ft). Admiralteyskaya's escalator is also one of the world's longest at 125 m (410 ft) long, pipped by Moscow's Park Pobedy station's escalator at 126.8 m (416 ft).

Sculpted figures in Narvskaya station

Off the Beaten Track

Gulf of Finland in winter

1 Gulf of Finland

Bordered by Finland, Estonia and Russia, the Gulf of Finland lies to the west of St Petersburg. Yelagin Island is a great spot from which to view it, especially in winter, when the Gulf freezes over and resembles an arctic wasteland.

2 Skate or Ski Across Yelagin Island

Krestovsky ostrov ■ Open 6am–11pm ■ Adm weekends only ■ www.nyphil.org

During the bitterly cold winter months, navigate Yelagin Island's frozen pathways on ice skates hired from its Central Park of Culture and Leisure, or traverse the arctic landscape on a pair of rented cross-country skis.

3 White Tulip Tower

Tikhoretskiy prospekt 21 ■ www.rtc.ru

Of particular interest to fans of Soviet architecture, the White Tulip Tower is located in the city's northern suburbs. Constructed in 1968 to house one of Russia's largest scientific research centres, it's among the country's most iconic Soviet buildings.

4 Summer Garden

Often overlooked by visitors, the lovely Summer Garden (see p73) was personally planned by Peter the Great in 1704 and restored by Catherine the Great after flood damage in 1777. It surrounds Peter's first Summer Palace and is adorned with 18th- and 19th-century sculptures and fountains.

5 Oranienbaum Park

Oranienbaum ■ Open 9am–8pm ■ www.peterhofmuseum.ru

This huge estate is 40 km west of St Petersburg. It is centred on the Great Palace built in the early 18th century by Prince Menshikov, Peter the Great's friend and confidante. Catherine the Great's extravagant Chinese Palace is in the Upper Park, which has canals, bridges and ponds.

Great Palace, Oranienbaum Park

6 Russian Railway Museum

Bibliotechnyi pereulok, 4, korpus 2 ■ 457 2316 ■ Open 10:30am–6pm Wed–Sun ■ Adm ■ www.rzd-museum.ru

The many exhibits on display at the fascinating, Russian Railway Museum include the only surviving steam locomotive of the C-series; an incredibly heavy railway artillery system with guns from the battleship "Empress Maria", which sunk in 1916; and a pre-revolutionary car, emblazoned with the Soviet red star, sporting authentic interiors.

Statue in the Summer Garden

Brightly coloured wall mural in the Street Art Museum

7 Street Art Museum
Shosse Revolyutsii 84 ■ 244 1494 ■ www.streetartmuseum.ru
Founded in 2011 after a graffiti party at a partially abandoned factory in the suburbs, the site's Soviet-era workshops are now adorned with massive wall-sized murals by street artists from all over the world. During the summer months, regular graffiti exhibitions are held in the complex's cavernous boiler room.

8 Hidden Passages
Behind the fine façades of some of central St Petersburg's 19th-century residential buildings are hidden courtyards reminiscent of Dostoevsky's *Crime and Punishment*, which are accessed by labyrinthine narrow passages. Opening times are unpredictable, but try to seek out the Mosaic Courtyard in Nab. Reki Fontanki 4, and the Wizard of Oz Courtyard in Ulitsa Pravdy 2–8.

9 Razliv Museum Centre
Ulitsa Yemelyanova 3, Razliv ■ 434 6145 ■ Open 11am–6pm Thu–Tue ■ Adm ■ www.razlivmuseum.spb.ru
Located some 40 km northwest of St Petersburg, Lenin's two historic hideouts – a wooden shed and a simple hut – have been left just the way they were when he used them to escape arrest in 1917. In the days of Communism the museum was often visited by school groups, but today there are very few tourists around.

10 Zhelyabova 25 Pyshechnaya (Doughnut Café)
Bolshaya Konushennaya ulitsa 25 ■ 314 0868 ■ Open 9am–8pm
Serving sweet coffee and sticky, hot doughnuts, this legendary café is about as close as you can get to an authentic experience of Soviet Russia. It has changed little since it opened in 1958 and has a resolutely retro interior.

Children's Attractions

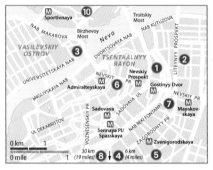

1 Circus

MAP P3 ■ Nab. Reki Fontanki 3
■ 570 5198 ■ Shows 3pm, 7pm ■ Adm

This is Russia's oldest circus, built in 1877. It puts on some of the country's best performances, and is a fun place to visit with children.

Performance at the Circus

2 Puppet Theatre

MAP E3 ■ Ulitsa Nekrasova 10
■ 273 6672 ■ Shows 11:30am, 3pm, 7pm ■ Adm

While the language barrier may make a lot of children's entertainment inaccessible, a performance at a puppet theatre poses no problems. The best is the Bolshoi Puppet Theatre, where shows are based around Russian fairy tales.

3 Zoological Museum

A superb attraction (see p91) for young and old alike, the sheer variety of specimens here, from dinosaurs to stuffed animals, is sure to capture the interest of children.

4 Grand Model of Russia Museum

Tsvetochnaya ulitsa 16
■ 495 5465 ■ Open 10am–8pm daily ■ Adm
■ www.grandmaket.ru

The Grandmaket Rossiya (Grand Model of Russia) features an 800-sq-m- (8,611-sq-ft-) miniature model of Russia on a 1:87 scale, depicting everything from rivers and mountains to bridges, ports, cities and villages. Children will enjoy pressing the buttons that activate the movement of objects such as trains.

5 Oceanarium

MAP D6 ■ Ulitsa Marata 86
■ 448 0077 ■ Open 10am–8pm
■ Adm ■ www.planeta-neptun.ru

Opened in 2006, St Petersburg's Oceanarium was the very first in Russia. It features over 4,500 species of fish, including sharks, and numerous squids. Children can watch the otters, seals and skates, and ride the travelator at the big auquarium. The souvenir shop has a large selection of mementoes and decorative shells.

6 Chocolate Museum

MAP L3 ■ Nevskiy prospekt 17
■ 315 1348 ■ Open 11am–9pm

Not a museum as such, the Chocolate Museum is a shop displaying and selling all manner of items crafted from chocolate. With lions, chessboards, Lenin and pop stars among the many creations, the Chocolate Museum is worth half an hour of anyone's time, especially people with children.

7 Children's Music Theatre

MAP P4 ■ Ulitsa Rubinshteyna 13 ■ 570 3346 ■ Call for timings ■ Adm ■ www.zazerkal.spb.ru

The musical theatre is another form of entertainment where the language barrier is easily overcome. Featuring performances of fairy tales, both Russian and foreign, and a musical version of Kipling's *Rikki-Tikki-Tavi*, the theatre's wonderful singers and scenery make this a real treat for adults as well as children.

⑧ Troika (Sleigh) ride at Shuvalovka

Sankt Petersburgskoe Shosse 111
■ **980 6580** ■ **Call for timings** ■ **Adm**
■ **www.russian-village.ru**

A winter ride through the thick snow on a *troika*, a traditional Russian sleigh led by horses, is an unforgettable experience. Rides can be booked at Shuvalovka, a replica Russian village that also offers a range of facilities, including a traditional Russian *banya* (sauna). Take a Peterhof bus from Avtovo metro station, and ask the driver to stop at Shuvalovka.

⑨ Boat Ride

In the summer months, a boat ride along the waterways *(see pp46–7)* is an excellent way to see the city. Children will enjoy being on the water, while adults can use the time to take in the magnificent architecture of the "Venice of the North". Boats collect passengers at many locations across the city.

The petting area at Leningrad Zoo

⑩ Leningrad Zoo

MAP C2 ■ **Aleksandrovskiy Park** ■ **232 8260** ■ **Open 10am–7pm Mon–Fri, 10am–9pm Sat–Sun** ■ **Adm**
■ **www.spbzoo.ru**

One of the world's northernmost zoos, the Leningrad Zoo (it retains the city's Soviet-era name) was opened in 1865. It contains a large number of attractions, from polar bears to a monkey-inhabited island. There are numerous special days throughout the year that celebrate different species.

Scenic boat ride on St Petersburg's waterways

⭐🔟 Entertainment

Gala concert featuring famous opera singers in Palace Square

1 Theatre

Russian speakers as well as theatre enthusiasts will find the performances a rewarding experience. Russia is the home of Stanislavsky (who pioneered the method acting approach) and playwrights such as Chekhov.

Performance of the *Golden Cockerel* opera at the Mariinskiy Theatre

2 Opera

The first opera performed in Russia was in 1731, while the first opera written in Russian was shown in 1755. The 19th century saw St Petersburg produce a number of opera greats such as Mikhail Glinka and Pyotr Tchaikovsky.

3 Classical Music

Famous Russian composers include Prokofiev, Stravinsky and Shostakovich. The latter's "Seventh Symphony", dedicated to the city of Leningrad, was premiered in 1942 during the siege of the city, and was defiantly broadcast through loadspeakers at the Nazi lines.

4 Cinema

The Soviet film industry suffered in post-*perestroika* Russia. However, it has since seen a revival. There are a few cinemas along Nevskiy prospekt, such as Aurora Cinema at No. 60. Khudozhestvenny at No. 67 is a good place to catch the latest Russian releases; for quirky arthouse films try Dom Kino at Karavannaya No. 12.

5 Ballet

Towards the end of the 17th century, Peter the Great invited foreign ballet instructors to teach in Russia. The art form has flourished in the country since, producing stars like Anna Pavlova and Rudolf Nureyev.

Ballet dancer in a production of *Le Corsaire*

6 Nightclubs

St Petersburg is second only to Moscow for its nightlife *(see p71)*. The city has clubs for every taste, from arty Fish Fabrique to the popular Purga.

7 Live Rock Music

St Petersburg was the birthplace of some of Russia's finest *perestroika*-era rock groups, including the enigmatic Kino. Venues like Fish Fabrique *(see p71)* and Griboedov *(see p105)* also host exciting new groups.

8 Football

St Petersburg's local team Zenit play at the Petrovskiy Stadium, and regularly feature in the Champions League. They also played at the Saint Petersburg Stadium *(see p98)* at the 2018 FIFA World Cup.

Zenit football match

9 Wandering "Piter"

St Petersburg, or "Piter", is a city made for walking *(see pp10–11)*. Wander up Nevskiy prospekt and along the city's canals and take a stroll during the "White Nights" in mid-summer, when the sun never fully sets. The city's sky-line is always impressive.

10 White Nights Festival

Running from May to July, this festival *(see p62)* of ballet, opera and classical music attracts hundreds of thousands of tourists. Scarlet Sails is a festival highlight, with ships cruising along the Neva amidst a terrific firework display.

TOP 10 VENUES FOR BALLET, OPERA, THEATRE AND CLASSICAL MUSIC

Mikhailovsky Theatre

1 Mikhaylovskiy Theatre
MAP N3 ▪ Ploshchad Iskusstv 1 ▪ 595 4305
Daily performances of opera and ballet.

2 Mariinskiy Theatre
A world-famous venue for ballet and opera *(see pp20–21)*.

3 Rimsky-Korsakov Conservatory
An opera, ballet and classical music venue *(see p82)*.

4 Octyabrsky Concert Hall
MAP F4 ▪ Ligovskiy prospekt 6 ▪ 275 1300
Matinees and evening performances of music shows, plays and ballets.

5 St Petersburg Opera
MAP B4 ▪ Galernaya ulitsa 33 ▪ 312 3982
Performances of less common works, such as 18th-century chamber operas.

6 Dom Kochnevoy
MAP P4 ▪ Nab. Reki Fontanki 41 ▪ 310 2987
A classical music venue on the bank of the Fontanka river.

7 Alexandriinsky Theatre
MAP N4 ▪ Pl Ostrovskovo 2 ▪ 312 2545
Theatre showing a wide range of plays, from Chekhov to modern playwrights.

8 Main Hall of the Shostakovich Philharmonia
MAP N3 ▪ Mikhaylovskaya ulitsa 2 ▪ 312 9871
A great place to see classical music.

9 Small Hall of the Shostakovich Philharmonia
MAP N3 ▪ Nevskiy prospekt 30 ▪ 571 8333
A charming 19th-century concert hall.

10 Academic Capella
MAP M2 ▪ Nab. Reki Moyki 20 ▪ 314 1058
A historic venue for classical concerts.

TOP 10 Russian Dishes

1 Kholodets
Despite its extremely unappetizing appearance, *kholodets* is a traditional Ukrainian dish that is incredibly popular all over Russia. It is made from meat picked off a boiling bone (traditionally pigs' trotters). As the meat cools, the gravy around it forms a kind of jelly. It is served with mustard or horseradish.

2 Caviar
Russia has two types of caviar. Black caviar is the more expensive of the two, and is roe from sturgeon. The red caviar, cheaper and far more common, is roe taken from salmon.

A bowl of *pelmeni*

3 Pelmeni
Pelmeni are like ravioli, only usually bigger. Served in a clear broth or with *smetana* (sour cream), they come in various shapes, sizes and prices. Avoid the cheaper versions, which often contain poor-quality meat.

4 Schi
Despite sounding like something that Dickens's orphan heroes would be forced to live on, this cabbage soup is actually a delicious, warming dish that should be tried at least once. It is a combination of meat, herbs and vegetables that has been popular for over 1,000 years.

Fish broth *ukha*

5 Ukha
Ukha is a very popular fish broth, usually prepared with salmon, pike or perch. As a rule, *ukha* should be made with a minimum of two different types of fish, and a maximum of four. It also often contains potatoes, onions and other vegetables.

6 Solyanka
The main ingredient of *solyanka* is pickled cucumber with brine. This is cooked, and then meat, fish or, occasionally, mushrooms are added to produce a delicious tangy-tasting soup.

7 Blini
Blini are buttery pancakes filled with anything from caviar to jam. You will find them on sale everywhere, from restaurants and cafés to street kiosks.

***Blini* with caviar**

8 Vareniki

Usually served as dessert, *vareniki* are boiled dumplings and are similar to *pelmeni*. They can be filled with potato and mushroom and accompanied with *smetana*, or eaten with sweeter fillings, such as cherry or curd. An excellent option for vegetarians in Russia, *vareniki* are lighter than *pelmeni*.

Sweet *vareniki* served with cherries

9 Borsch

A staple Russian/Ukrainian dish, the St Petersburg *borsch* is a filling beetroot-based soup usually prepared with meat, although vegetarian versions can also be found. A thick *borsch* tastes delicious with *smetana*.

Borsch* with *smetana

10 Okroshka

Okroshka is another Russian cold soup which contains an unlikely combination of ingredients – cucumber, spring onion, boiled eggs, ham and *kvas (see Drinks, opposite)*. It is a refreshing summer soup found everywhere in Russia. Many families have their own secret recipes.

TOP 10 DRINKS

Traditional *kefir*

1 Kefir
A nutritious, fermented milk drink that originated in the Northern Caucasus mountains.

2 Vodka
The national drink, its name is derived from *voda*, the Russian word for water.

3 Ryazhenka
A sweet-tasting, fermented, baked milk drink with many health benefits.

4 Local Beer
Vasileostrovakoe, Baltica, Botchkarev and Nevskoe are local lagers of varying strength.

5 Kvas
A slightly alcoholic (less than 1%) drink made from fermented rye and barley.

6 "Soviet Champagne"
Though officially "Russian sparkling", and despite the USSR not having existed for years, most people still refer to this drink as "Soviet champagne", in defiance of rulings making it illegal to call sparkling wine "champagne" unless it comes from that region of France.

7 Mors
A traditional Russian juice drink, *mors* is a red, vitamin-packed mixture of water and cranberry or lingberry juice.

8 Samogon
The local equivalent of hooch or moonshine – you may be offered some of this if you visit rural areas.

9 Tea
Tea was introduced to Russia in 1600. It is sometimes drunk with a lemon or fruit preserve, but rarely with milk.

10 Georgian Wine
A very popular wine, but supplies are often erratic due to Russia's dispute with Georgia.

🔟 Russian Restaurants

 Idiot
When Idiot (see p76) first opened, its vegetarian menu proved an immediate hit with the local expat community. It serves meat-free versions of Russian food, from *borsch* to *pelmeni*.

Warm interior of Mari Vanna

 Mari Vanna
This cosy Russian restaurant (see p99) offers great views of the city's major sights. The interior is decorated with traditional Russian scarves and handmade lamp shades. The menu offers authentic Russian cuisine such as *shchi* (cabbage soup), golden *pirozhki* (baked buns with fillings), as well as *Guriyev blini* (pancakes). Make sure to try the national staple of buckwheat *kasha* (porridge) as well as the sturgeon or pike caviar.

 Teplo
With its name translating as "warmth", Teplo (see p77) is a homely restaurant. It serves Russian favourites as well as Italian classics. Try the vegetarian dishes such as pumpkin soup, cold *borsch* (beetroot soup) or fried eggplant with mozzarella and tomatoes. There is an outdoor as well as an indoor play area for kids, along with board games and kicker.

 Literary Café
Centrally located, this café (see p76) is famous as the place where the national poet Pushkin (see p46) met his love rival before setting off for the duel in which he would lose his life. The café, it must be said, has made the most of this historical hook, and its food, while perfectly edible, is not as memorable as the ideal setting.

 Russian Empire
Containing four separate dining rooms, and set in what was once a part of the Stroganov Palace (see p13), Russian Empire (see p76) is a throwback to the time of the tsars. With 19th-century armagnacs and delicious food served on Versace porcelain plates, this restaurant offers perhaps the most extravagant dining experience in the whole of Russia.

6 Kvartirka
A Soviet-themed café (see p70), Kvartirka's name translates as "happiness". Enjoy the hearty Russian fare that is served with a smile. The café also specializes in a *samovar* tea service, which is accompanied by a mouth-watering assortment of Russian pastries and jams. The place can be quite busy during rush hour, so book in advance.

Interior of Russian Vodka Room No. 1

⑦ Russian Vodka Room No. 1

The name of this place says it all. Authentic Russian dishes, such as *ukha* and *blinis (see p56)*, feature on the menu, along with a variety of pickles traditionally eaten with vodka, such as salted cabbage, gherkins and pickled mushrooms. The restaurant *(see p83)* serves 213 different types of vodka, and there is even an on-site vodka museum.

⑧ Palkin

Founded in 1785, Palkin *(see p70)* has long been the haunt of some of the city's finest writers, including Dostoevsky and Gogol *(see p46)*. Superb, traditional "Imperial Russia" cuisine – venison dumplings with sour cream, for example – shares the menu with more modern, cosmopolitan creations. The service is impeccable, and the restaurant is also home to a permanent display of local art.

⑨ Astoria Restaurant

Located in the luxurious Astoria Hotel, Astoria Restaurant *(see p76)* offers top-quality international and Russian cuisine, including imaginative black and red caviar dishes to rival those found at the Belmond Grand Hotel Europe. The exquisite surroundings are steeped in history – Hitler, grossly underestimating Russian resilience, is said to have planned his victory bash in the Winter Gardens here following the fall of Leningrad.

⑩ L'Europe

Located within the sumptuous Belmond Grand Hotel Europe, this Art Deco marvel is one of the city's top spots for people-watching and sampling some of the best food in town *(see p70)*. The house special – truffle-scented scrambled egg topped with caviar set within an empty eggshell – is a decadent classic.

The opulent dining room at L'Europe

Souvenirs

A selection of *matryoshka* dolls

the booming tourist demand, there are some fine, original Lenin statues on sale at the Souvenir Market near the Church on Spilled Blood. Notes, coins and badges commemorating achievements of the communist system are usually genuine.

4 Russian Music

From choral church music and the *perestroika*-era rock of Kino to the modern-day sounds of Leningrad, old CDs and vinyls of Russian music make excellent souvenirs. The best shops are on and near Nevskiy prospekt. Prices usually range from ₽200 to ₽400.

5 Caviar

Black or red caviar makes a great gift. Spread thinly on bread, its distinctive taste is not easily forgotten. It is best to buy caviar in large supermarkets, after carefully checking the expiry date.

6 Vodka

The range of vodka on offer here, from cheap rot-gut to grandly packaged brands, is vast. Stolichnaya and Gzelhka are long-established brands and anything over ₽200 is almost certain to be safe. Always buy from a supermarket.

1 Matryoshka Dolls

Consisting of a series of carved dolls, each one smaller than the next, *matryoshka* dolls are on sale all over the city and come in a variety of styles. The traditional ones are the prettiest, but those painted as Russian, Soviet and world leaders are also very popular.

2 Gzhel Porcelain

Gzhel porcelain has been produced in Gzhel, an area not far from Moscow, since the middle of the 18th century. The distinctive blue and white patterned ceramics are extremely popular. The Gzhel style is also used in traditional Russian art.

3 Soviet Memorabilia

While authentic Soviet memorabilia is difficult to find, with factories turning out modern reproductions to meet

7 Samovar

The samovar is traditionally used to boil water for tea. Made of brass or copper, and warmed by coals contained in the central tube, the vessel was designed in the 18th century. The word is a combination of *"samo"*, meaning "itself", and *"varit"*, meaning "to boil". A permit is required to export a samovar made before 1945.

Traditional samovar

Palekh box

⑧ Palekh Box
These bright hand-painted boxes originated in the 18th century in the village of Palekh. Featuring scenes from Russian fairy tales, battle scenes or copies of works of art, they range from expensive masterpieces to cheaper, assembly-line-produced ones.

⑨ Chess Sets
Russia has long been famed for its chess *(shakhmaty)* and chess sets are available in a variety of styles. These range from the more modest options costing around ₽500 to handmade sets that can go for up to ₽2,500 and higher.

Russian chess set

⑩ Amber Jewellery
The Baltic Sea coast holds around 90 per cent of the world's extractable amber. The region is renowned for jewellery and other souvenirs created from this fossilized tree resin. Some pieces contain tiny insects and fragments of plants that were trapped in the resin around 50 million years ago.

TOP 10 BEST SHOPS

1 Gostinyy Dvor Mall
MAP D4 ▪ Nevsky prospekt 35
One of the world's oldest shopping arcades, with over 300 stores.

2 Dom Knigi
MAP D4 ▪ Nevsky prospekt 28
The city's top bookstore is set in Singer House, a striking Art Nouveau building.

3 Yeliseev's
MAP D4 ▪ Nevskiy prospekt 56
A renowned food store mentioned in Tolstoy's *Anna Karenina*, with huge stained-glass windows.

4 Grand Palace Boutiques Gallery
MAP D4 ▪ Nevsky prospekt 44
Expensive boutiques located in a palatial shopping centre.

5 Taiga
MAP C3 ▪ Palace Embankment
Hip boutiques and businesses within a stylishly restored old mansion.

6 Nevskiy Centre
MAP E4 ▪ Nevsky prospekt 116
Best known for the Finnish Stockmann department store, the city's largest.

7 Imperial Porcelain
www.imperial-porcelain.com
Russia's oldest porcelain manufacturer.

8 Northway
MAP C3 ▪ Palace Embankment
A fantastic selection of *matryoshki* and typical Russian souvenirs.

9 Erarta
A good spot to purchase contemporary Russian artworks *(see p92)*.

10 Passazh
MAP D4 ▪ Nevsky prospekt 48
This chic 19th-century department store is housed under a vast glass roof.

Passazh department store

St Petersburg for Free

1 The Hermitage
On the first Thursday of the month entry to the Hermitage *(see pp14–17)* is free during the usual opening hours of 10:30am to 6pm. Arrive early to beat the queues in high season as the free day is popular with both locals and tourists.

2 Cruiser Aurora
Commissioned in 1903, this 127-m (417-ft) steam-powered cruiser *(see p95)* is most famous for its role at the beginning of Russia's 1917 Revolution, when sailors on board fired a blank shot as the signal for the Bolsheviks to storm St Petersburg's Winter Palace. After extensive restoration work, it reopened to the public free of charge in 2016.

3 Mikhaylovskiy Gardens
MAP P2 ▪ Open May–Sep: 10am–10pm; Oct–Mar: 10am–8pm ▪ Closed Apr
The scenic parkland surrounding Mikhaylovskiy Castle *(see p69)* offers welcome respite from the sights of bustling central St Petersburg.

4 Alexander Nevskiy Monastery
There's no charge to explore this 18th-century monastery complex *(see p102)*, the final resting place of the city's patron saint, Alexander Nevskiy.

Palace in Yelagin Island

5 Yelagin Island
Once the exclusive preserve of wealthy aristocrats, this delightful park is dotted with picturesque lakes and is free to enter on weekdays. Its westernmost point is a great spot to watch the sun set over the Gulf of Finland *(see p50)*.

6 White Nights Festival
The White Nights Festival runs from May to July, when the sun barely sets due to the city's position just a few degrees south of the Arctic Circle. It's St Petersburg's busiest time of year, so accommodation should be booked well in advance, but many of the festival events are free. Numerous carnivals with participants in period costumes and the Scarlet Sails celebration – fireworks, music concerts and a massive water show – are among the highlights.

Alexander Nevskiy Monastery

7 Explore the Metro

Great for a rainy day, the older stations of St Petersburg's Metro system (see pp48–9) are elegantly decorated with stunning mosaics, murals and sculptures celebrating Soviet achievements; newer stations are more functional yet often have bold design features.

8 Opening the Bridges

Between May and November, the city's many drawbridges are raised for several hours after midnight to allow the passage of river traffic. The spectacle of their opening draws crowds, especially during the White Nights Festival, but be sure you're on the right side before they open as it essentially splits the city in two.

Opening the bridges

9 Beaches

St Petersburg's most popular central beach (see p98) lies on the Neva river side of the Peter and Paul Fortress. Packed with sunbathers on sunny summer days, the narrow sandy strip has wonderful city views.

10 Free Tour

www.petersburgfreetour.com

The St Petersburg Free Tour covers most of the city's must-see sights and runs every day from 10:45am. Most tours take around 2 hours and 30 minutes. While completely free in theory, it's customary to tip the professional guides if you're satisfied. Popular and highly rated, places should be booked in advance online.

TOP 10 BUDGET TIPS

Bike hire station

1 If the weather permits, hiring a bike can be a cost-effective way to navigate the city. Velobayk (www.velobike.ru) is a network of rental stations dotted across the city.

2 Stay in an apartment with self-catering facilities to cut down on meal costs.

3 Get a Russian pay-as-you-go SIM card for cheaper local calls and internet data on your mobile phone.

4 Buy a St Petersburg Card (www.petersburgcard.com) valid for 2, 3, 5 or 7 days. It gives free access to many of the city's top sights.

5 Make lunch the main meal of your day. Many high-end restaurants offer great-value "business lunches" between 12pm and 4pm.

6 To qualify for student discounts across a number of St Petersburg's sights and attractions, students will need to get an ISIC card before they go.

7 If you are staying in St Petersburg for longer than a week, consider buying a metro travel card for discounted fares.

8 It's much cheaper to make a single large ATM cash withdrawal rather than several small ones as Russian banks will usually charge a fixed fee per transaction.

9 Become a couchsurfer at www.couchsurfing.com and find free local accommodation.

10 Many of the events during the White Nights Festival are free, but do be aware that hotel prices at this time (from late May until July) are sky-high. Be sure to book well in advance for the best rates. Short-stay apartments may be a good option during this period.

St Petersburg
Area by Area

Statue of Alexander Pushkin silhouetted
against the Russian Museum

⭐10 Gostinyy Dvor

The city's commercial, social and cultural centre displays the paradoxical character of the "Venice of the North", with modern shopping centres standing next to tsarist-era churches and 18th-century Style-Moderne wonders. From the bustle of Nevskiy prospekt and Ploshchad Vosstaniya to the secluded Arts Square, Gostinyy Dvor is a microcosm of Russia today and a reminder of the city's rich cultural heritage.

Interior of a dome in the Church on Spilled Blood

① Church on Spilled Blood
Despite its typically "Russian" onion domes, this church *(see pp18–19)* is an anomaly in St Petersburg, a city more famous for its European-style architecture. It is an example of Russia's Eastern cultural heritage. Though the façade is undergoing restoration until 2025, the mosaic interiors are still open to public.

GOSTINYY DVOR

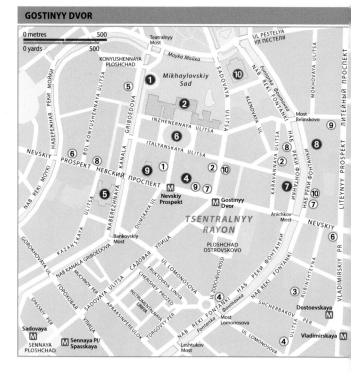

Restaurant, **a painting by Pavel Filonov in the Russian Museum**

2 Russian Museum

This museum's exhibits *(see pp22–3)* explore the history of Russian art from 13th-century icons to modern masterpieces. It contains works by perhaps the greatest of the city's avant-garde painters, Pavel Filonov, an artist little known in the West, but who is reported to be President Putin's favourite. For those with more traditional tastes, the museum also displays canvases by landscape painter Ivan Shishkin, another St Petersburg artist.

3 Ploshchad Vosstaniya
MAP E4

The vast, imposing Ploshchad Vosstaniya, or Uprising Square, gets its name from the events of February 1917, when a group of Russian soldiers refused to fire upon demonstrators, instead taking up arms on the side of the discontented masses. In 1985, it was the scene of a walkabout by the Soviet leader Mikhail Gorbachev, who went into the masses to discuss the country's problems.

4 Armenian Church
MAP N3 ■ Nevskiy prospekt 40–42 ■ 570 4108 ■ Open 9am–8pm

While today a beautifully decorated building, during the Soviet era and the period immediately after *perestroika* the Armenian Church *(see p12)* lay in ruins, abandoned to the elements. It was handed back to the Armenian community in the mid-1990s. With the help of funds from the vast Armenian diaspora as well as local donations, the church was restored to its former glory.

Façade of the Armenian Church

5 Cathedral of Our Lady of Kazan

MAP M3 ■ Kazansky ploshchad 2 ■ 314 4663 ■ Open 8:30am–end of evening service daily (from 6:30am Sat & Sun)

This building *(see p13)* was constructed in 1811 solely for housing Russian Orthodoxy's precious, miracle-working icon, Our Lady of Kazan. After the 1917 Revolution, the icon was seized by the atheist Soviet authorities. It resurfaced many years later in New York and is once again housed in the cathedral.

6 Arts Square

MAP N3 ■ Ploshchad Iskusstv

Dominated by a commanding statue of Pushkin, Arts Square is a showpiece for the city's cultural institutions and a patch of green among the canals and grand constructions of Gostinyy Dvor. Designed by Carlo Rossi in the early 19th century, it is not far from the Philharmonia Concert Hall, the Russian Museum, the Circus and Mikhaylovskiy Castle.

A rare egg in the Fabergé Museum

7 Fabergé Museum

MAP D4 ■ Nab. Reki Fontanki 21 ■ 333 2655 ■ Open 10am–9pm Sat–Thu ■ www.fabergemuseum.ru

Opened in 2013 to exhibit Russian billionaire Viktor Vekselberg's collection of over 4,000 pieces of Russian art, the museum *(see p45)* occupies the grand 18th-century Shuvalov Palace. Its highlights are the nine rare Fabergé eggs Vekselberg purchased for $100 million from the collection of American newspaper magnate Malcolm Forbes in 2004.

8 Sheremetev Palace

MAP P3 ■ Nab. Reki Fontanki 34 ■ 272 4441 ■ Open 11am–7pm Thu–Mon, 1–9pm Wed (closed last Fri of month) ■ Adm

This elegant Baroque palace, built in 1750, was originally the residence of the wealthy Sheremetev family. During the Soviet period, one of the attached communal flats was the home of Anna Akhmatova *(see p47)*, who lived here for nearly 30 years. The palace is now a museum dedicated to musical instruments.

PUSHKIN'S AFRICAN PAST

Alexander Pushkin *(see p46)*, whose statue stands in Arts Square, was the great-grandson of African slave Abram Hannibal, brought to Russia by Peter the Great. Hannibal gained popularity around the court of the tsar and served as the governor of Tallinn (then known as Reval). Pushkin, who owed his distinctive curly hair to Hannibal, even began a novel (unfinished) about him.

Cathedral of Our Lady of Kazan

A DAY AROUND NEVSKIY PROSPEKT

Church on Spilled Blood

Russian Museum

nab. Kanala Griboedova

Arts Square

Nevskiy prospekt

Church of St Catherine

L'Europe

Armenian Church

Brynza

Cathedral of Our Lady of Kazan

▶ **MORNING**

Starting around 11am to avoid the morning rush-hour crowds, turn right from the even-numbered side of **Nevskiy prospekt** *(see pp12–13)* into the atmospheric nab. Kanala Griboedova. From here, walk down to the **Church on Spilled Blood** *(see pp18–19)* at the end of the canal and then walk back up to the exhibition halls of the **Russian Museum** *(see pp22–3)*, where you can feast your eyes upon one of the world's best collections of Russian art. Afterwards, weather permitting, picnic at the nearby **Arts Square**, an oasis of calm in this bustling area. If the weather is bad, then savour some delicious pancakes in the Russian Museum café on the ground floor.

AFTERNOON

Walk back up nab. Kanala Griboedova and cross Nevskiy prospekt at the traffic lights opposite the metro station. To your right is the **Cathedral of Our Lady of Kazan**, inspired by St Peter's in Rome. Heading away from the cathedral, take a stroll along Nevskiy prospekt, visiting a few souvenir shops. Be sure to stop by at the brooding **Church of St Catherine** and the "Blue Pearl of Nevskiy Prospekt" – the **Armenian Church** *(see p67)*. Then head to the Grand Hotel Europe, and splash out on a meal at the stunning **L'Europe** restaurant *(see p70)*. If your wallet won't quite stretch to this, make your way to the nearby **Brynza** *(see p70)* for tasty traditional Russian food.

⑨ **Church of St Catherine**
MAP N3 ▪ Nevskiy prospekt 30
▪ Open 9am–9pm

Built in 1782, the Church of St Catherine is the oldest Roman Catholic church in Russia *(see p13)*. It saw many state funerals in pre-revolutionary Russia, including that of the last king of Poland, who was one of Catherine the Great's many lovers, and those of the heroes of the 1812 war against Napoleon.

⑩ **Mikhaylovskiy Castle**
MAP P2 ▪ Inzhenernaya ulitsa 4
▪ 595 4248 ▪ Open 10am–6pm Mon, Wed & Fri–Sun, 1–9pm Thu
▪ Adm

This castle was constructed for Paul I in 1797–1801. The tsar's fear of being assassinated led him to surround the castle with moats and drawbridges, as well as build a secret escape tunnel. Despite all this, the tsar was murdered after just 40 days in his new residence. Today it is a branch of the nearby Russian Museum.

Entrance to Mikhaylovskiy Castle

See map on pp66–7 ←

Restaurants

PRICE CATEGORIES
For a three-course meal for one with half
a bottle of wine, taxes and extra charges.

₽ under ₽4,000 ₽₽ ₽4,000–8,000
₽₽₽ over ₽8,000

L'Europe
MAP N3 ▪ Mikhaylovskaya
ulitsa 1/7 ▪ 329 6630 ▪ ₽₽

L'Europe boasts some of the finest
food in St Petersburg, along with an
extensive wine and cognac list. The
Sunday brunch is excellent.

2 Tarkhun
MAP P3 ▪ Karavannaya ulitsa
14 ▪ 571 1115 ▪ ₽

This elegant Georgian restaurant
combines Western European service
and style with some of Southern
Russia's most intriguing dishes.

3 Kvartirka
MAP E4 ▪ Nevskiy prospekt 51
▪ 315 5561 ▪ Open noon–1am ▪ ₽

After shopping, visit this cosy café
where hearty Russian fare is served.

4 Fiolet
MAP D5 ▪ Ploschad
Lomonosova 4 ▪ 407 5207 ▪ ₽

An Asian fusion restaurant set in a
minimalist dining room, Fiolet's broad
menu focuses on fresh seafood.

5 Baklazhan
MAP E5 ▪ Galeriya Mall,
Ligovskiy prospekt 30 ▪ 640 1616 ▪ ₽

With lovely city views, Baklazhan has
a reputation for superb Caucasian
and Uzbek cuisine, including good
vegetarian options.

6 Palkin
MAP E4 ▪ Nevskiy prospekt 47
▪ 703 5371 ▪ ₽₽

One of the city's top restaurants has
President Putin as a notable patron.
In a 19th-century-style interior,
Palkin offers white-gloved service
and a menu of exquisitely presented
Russian and international dishes.

7 Brynza
MAP N3 ▪ Nevskiy prospekt
50A ▪ 944 4490 ▪ ₽

This restaurant is renowned for its
delicious *chebureki* (traditional deep-
fried pasties), which come filled with
salmon, meat, mushrooms or cheese.

8 Marketplace
MAP M3 ▪ Nevskiy prospekt 24
▪ 854 4833 ▪ ₽

A popular budget eatery with an open
kitchen and a homely rustic interior.
Steamed organic trout and mutton
kebab are on the eclectic menu.

9 Konditerskaya Sever
MAP N3 ▪ Nevskiy prospekt 44
▪ 571 2589 ▪ ₽

Opposite Gostinyy Dvor, this
patisserie and café serves a mind-
boggling choice of cakes and buns
at surprisingly reasonable prices.

10 Tsar
MAP N4 ▪ Sadovaya ulitsa 12
▪ 640 1616 ▪ ₽₽

The opulent surroundings and
gourmet Russian cuisine at Tsar
ensure that an evening spent here
will be a night to remember.

Elegant interior at Tsar

Clubs and Bars

Quirky seating area at Fish Fabrique

1 Fish Fabrique
MAP E5 ■ Ligovskiy prospekt
53 ■ 764 4857 ■ Concerts start at 9pm
■ Adm
A legendary St Petersburg venue,
Fish Fabrique puts on fantastic
live concerts and club nights.

2 Bar Cuba Libre
MAP N3 ■ Sadovaya ulitsa 7-9-
11 ■ 983 5526 ■ Open 24 hours a day
This place offers about 200 cocktails
and some tasty snacks at reasonable
prices, as well as music and dancing.

3 Schastye
MAP D5 ■ Rubinshteina ulitsa,
15/17 ■ 572 2675
Serving Russian and European
cuisine, this bar and restaurant
offers a warm atmosphere. Book
in advance to avoid the rush hours.

4 Bekitzer
MAP N3 ■ Rubinshteina ulitsa,
40/11 ■ 926 4342
The interior of this bar is decorated
with Tel-Aviv-style graffiti. Try Israeli
steet food – falafel, kebab and hum-
mus – paired with unique cocktails.

5 Mod Club
MAP L4 ■ Nab. Kanala
Griboedova 7 ■ 728 0998
■ Open Sun–Thu: 2pm–midnight,
Fri & Sat: 6pm–6am ■ Adm
Popular with students, this hip club
offers live music and DJ sets, and
features up-and-coming Russian acts.

6 Biblioteka
MAP M3 ■ Nevskiy prospekt 20
■ 244 1594
Set above a café and restaurant, is a
top-floor bar at this fashionable spot.
The building is also home to a florist
and a number of bookshops.

7 Mishka Bar
MAP P4 ■ Nab. Reki Fontanki
40 ■ 643 2550 ■ Open Sun–Thu:
6pm–2am, Fri & Sat: 6pm–5am
A funky spot that is packed with
hipsters at weekends. Expect disco
or retro tunes and cheap cocktails.

8 Purga
MAP P3 ■ Nab. Reki Fontanki 11
■ 570 5123 ■ Adm
Purga is actually two nightclubs in
one, located right next to each other
on the bank of the Fontanka. It is
famous for its Soviet-style nightly
celebrations of New Year's Eve.

9 Terminal Bar
MAP E4 ■ Belinskogo Ulitsa 11
■ 939 6123
A version of the infamous New York
den, this US/Russian-owned bar has
simple decor and a trendy vibe.

10 PirO.G.I.
MAP P4 ■ Nab. Reki Fontanki 40
■ 275 3558 ■ Open 24 hours a day
This café/club offers an intimate
environment for poetry readings and
young musicians. It also has a book-
shop and has good set-price lunches.

See map on pp66–7

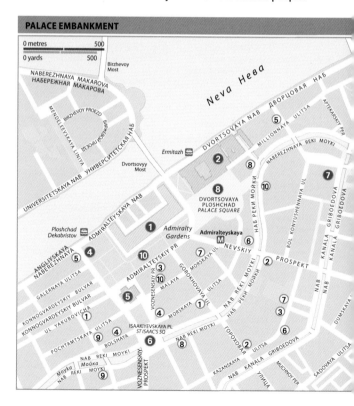 Palace Embankment

Unlike nearby Gostinyy Dvor, Palace Embankment contains very little in the way of shops and restaurants. Dominated instead by the symbols of Imperial, pre-revolutionary Russia, this is a particularly elegant area of the city. It showcases the splendour of the Winter Palace – the former residence of the tsars, now part of the stunning Hermitage – as well as the colossal St Isaac's Cathedral and the embodiment of imperial strength that is the Bronze Horseman statue. A stroll here highlights the sheer weight of history contained in this city of just under five million people.

The Bronze Horseman

PALACE EMBANKMENT

1 The Admiralty
MAP K3

■ Admiralteyskaya nab. 2
■ Closed to public

Immediately after founding St Petersburg, Peter the Great set about building a navy powerful enough to repel any attack on the city and expand Russia's regional ambitions. The Admiralty, built between 1704–11, was originally the shipyard where Russia's first battleships were produced. From 1806 to 1623, the Admiralty was rebuilt by the architect Andrey Zakharov, who decorated its 407-m (1,335-ft) wide façade with potent symbols of Russia's now-powerful fleet.

A gallery in the Hermitage

2 The Hermitage
The famous Hermitage (see pp14–17), which consists of five separate buildings, is one of the world's largest museums. Its enormous and breathtaking collection, containing works by Michelangelo, Leonardo da Vinci, Picasso and Rembrandt, is far too large to see in a single day. The New Hermitage is the only purpose-built museum within the complex.

3 Summer Garden
MAP N1 ■ Letniy sad ■ Open Oct–Mar: 10am–8pm Wed–Mon (May–Sep: to10pm) ■ Closed Apr

This garden was the pet project of Peter the Great (see p38), who spared no expense to create a botanical wonderland, complete with imported trees and plants. Peter's Summer Garden was destroyed in a flood in 1777, and the English-style garden that exists today was commissioned by Catherine the Great. It features a bronze statue of Russian 19th-century fable writer Ivan Krylov, sculpted by Pyotr Klodt in 1854. The biggest draw is the garden's fountains, which represent scenes from Aesop's Fables.

4 Decembrist's Square
MAP K3

Dominated by the Bronze Horseman, Peter the Great astride a horse, this square was the site of an attempted coup by officers of the Russian army on 14 December 1825, during the inauguration of Nicholas I.

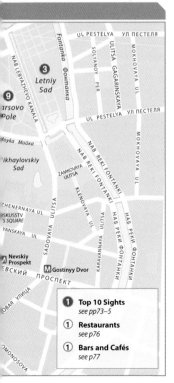

NAB LEBYAZHEVO KANALA
Fontanka Фонтанка
UL PESTELYA УЛ ПЕСТЕЛЯ
SOLYANOY PER
ULITSA GAGARINSKAYA
MOKHOVAYA UL
3 Letniy Sad
9
arsovo Pole
UL PESTELYA УЛ ПЕСТЕЛЯ
МОХОВАЯ УЛ
Иoyka Мойка
NAB REKI FONTANKI
NAB REKI FONTANKI
МОКHOVAYA UL
ikhaylovskiy Sad
ZAMKOVAYA ULITSA
KLENOVAYA UL
KARAVANNAYA ULITSA
НАБ РЕКИ ФОНТАНКИ
НАБ РЕКИ ФОНТАНКИ
HENERNAYA UL
SKUSSTV
S SQUARE
YANSKAYA UL
SADOVAYA UL
M Nevskiy Prospekt
ЕВСКИЙ Gostinyy Dvor
ПРОСПЕКТ
ПРОСПЕКТ
ЮВАЯ УЛИЦА
OMONOSOVA

1 Top 10 Sights
see pp73–5

1 Restaurants
see p76

1 Bars and Cafés
see p77

Interior of St Isaac's Cathedral

THE BRONZE HORSEMAN

At the edge of the Admiralty Gardens is The Bronze Horseman, an 18th-century statue of tsar and founder of St Petersburg, Peter the Great. It acquired its name after an 1833 poem by Pushkin about a man called Yevgeny who loses his sweetheart during the flood of 1824. Yevgeny blames Peter the Great in anger, and the statue comes to life and chases him to his death.

5 St Isaac's Cathedral

St Isaac's Cathedral (see pp28–9), a captivating edifice sil-houetted against the St Petersburg sky, stands at the edge of St Isaac's Square. The church's interior is lavishly decorated with marble and other semi-precious stones, and the upper sections of the exterior are adorned with masterfully sculpted figures of saints and angels.

6 St Isaac's Square

MAP K4 ■ Isaakiyevskaya ploshchad

St Isaac's Square was used as a marketplace in the 19th century. It is surrounded by a great number of St Petersburg's most famous buildings and monuments, including the striking St Isaac's Cathedral, the Astoria Hotel and the Mariinskiy Palace, which houses the St Petersburg City Hall. Also at the square

is Pyotr Klodt's statue of Nicholas I, who took Russia into the Crimean War. The reliefs on the pedestal depict events from his 30-year reign. St Isaac's Square features in Gogol's (see p46) famous short story "The Overcoat".

7 Museum of Soviet Arcade Machines

MAP K3 ■ Konyushennayha ploschad, 2 B ■ Open 11am–8pm daily ■ Adm

This recreation of a 1980s Soviet gaming arcade has over 60 arcade games that visitors can play using old 15 kopek coins. It's thought that when Soviet leader Nikita Khrushchev travelled to the US in 1959, he was so impressed with arcade games he ordered Soviet military factories to reproduce them in line with Marxist ideology, leading to games focused on strength and hand-eye coordination rather than fantasies.

8 Palace Square

The city is famed for its wide open spaces, vast squares and never-ending embankments. Palace Square (see p14) perfectly encapsulates the sense of overwhelming expansive-nesses one gets when walking the city's streets. Flanked by the

Majestic Palace Square

Hermitage and the 19th-century General Staff Building, which houses the Hermitage's Impressionist and Post-Impressionist collection, Palace Square has witnessed many historical events over the years, including the massacre of "Bloody Sunday" *(see p38)*. Before the Revolution, it was the setting for military parades, often led by the tsar on horseback. It is still a venue for political meetings and public events like rock concerts.

Eternal Flame monument

9 Field of Mars
MAP N1 ■ Marsovo Pole

This area, named after the Roman god of war, was used in the 19th century for military manoeuvres and parades. Reclaimed from swampland and extensively drained, it earned the nickname "Sahara of St Petersburg". A popular spot with locals during spring, it contains the Eternal Flame monument (1957), dedicated to those who died during the 1917 Revolution *(see p38)*, and the Monument to Revolutionary Fighters (1917–19), designed by Lev Rudnev.

10 Admiralty Gardens
MAP K3 ■ Aleksandrovskiy sad

In winter, the Admiralty Gardens transform into a winter wonderland, with mounds of snow filling the ornamental fountain. In summer they are full of relaxing office-workers, students and chess players. The gardens look directly onto the Admiralty *(see p73)*, and are full of busts of famous Russian composers and writers, including the ubiquitous Gogol *(see p46)*, and the 19th-century composer, Mikhail Glinka.

A DAY OF IMPERIAL WONDERS

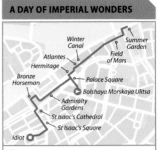

> **MORNING**

Turn off the even-numbered side of Nevskiy prospekt and walk down Bolshaya Morskaya ulitsa, sticking to the left. An unforgettable view of the **Hermitage** and **Palace Square** *(see pp14–15)* will open up in front of you. Stroll through the vastness of the square, examining the colossal, freestanding **Alexander Column** *(see p15)* as you do so. Before entering the Hermitage, wander over to the **Atlantes** *(see p14)* and the **Winter Canal** *(see p41)*. It is impossible to see everything the Hermitage has to offer in one visit, and the scale of the collections can get overwhelming, so it's best to take a break after a couple of hours. Have lunch at the museum café or, if the weather is good, have a picnic in the nearby **Summer Garden** *(see p73)* or **Field of Mars**.

AFTERNOON

After lunch, head away from the river, crossing Palace Square again towards **St Isaac's Square**. Pass through the **Admiralty Gardens** to look at busts of Russian composers and writers, and pay a visit to the Bronze Horseman, a local landmark. The gardens are a popular spot for taking wedding photographs. Turn away from the embankment, and head for St Isaac's Square, where the statue of Nicholas I stands. Next, climb the many steps to the top of the massive **St Isaac's Cathedral** *(see pp28–9)* for a great view of the city. Later, walk back across St Isaac's Square to **Idiot** *(see p76)* for a relaxing meal.

See map on pp72–3 ◄

Restaurants

1 Clean Plates Society
MAP L4 ■ Gorokhovaya ulitsa 13 ■ 934 9764 ■ ₽

Small and friendly, this trendy spot offers some of the city's best burgers and salads at bargain prices.

Interior of Clean Plates Society

2 Russian Empire
MAP M3 ■ Nevskiy prospekt 17 ■ 571 2409 ■ ₽₽

Occupying three lavishly appointed rooms of the splendid 18th-century Stroganoff Palace, this is the place to go to dine like tsars and tsarinas.

3 Tandoor
MAP K3 ■ Admiralteyskiy prospekt 10 ■ 312 3886 ■ ₽

This is one of the few places in the city that serves authentic Indian food, with superb flavours. The spice level can be adjusted to suit individual palates.

4 Astoria Restaurant
MAP K4 ■ Hotel Astoria, Bolshaya Morskaya ulitsa 39 ■ 494 5815 ■ ₽₽

One of the city's top restaurants, this has a varied Russian menu with a French touch. It offers wonderful views of St Isaac's Cathedral.

5 Da Albertone
MAP M1 ■ Millionnaya ulitsa 23 ■ 315 8673 ■ ₽

This pizzeria is a great place to grab a bite to eat after exploring the collections of the nearby Hermitage.

6 Literary Café
MAP L3 ■ Nevsky prospekt 18 ■ 312 6057 ■ ₽

Evoking a 19th-century atmosphere, this restaurant offers Russian as well as European dishes.

7 Bushe
MAP L3 ■ Malaya Morskaya ulitsa 7 ■ 315 5371 ■ ₽

This very popular French bakery and café is one of the city's best spots for sandwiches made with rustic loaves. There's also delicious cakes, coffee and a great choice of teas.

8 La Russ
MAP C3 ■ Nab. Reki Moyki 37 ■ 571 7591 ■ ₽

This over-the-top Russian-style cabaret-restaurant may be a bit kitschy, but the food and performers are top-notch.

9 Idiot
MAP K5 ■ Nab. Reki Moyki 82 ■ 315 1675 ■ ₽

This vegetarian restaurant is a St Petersburg favourite, renowned for its excellent business lunches. All guests are given a free shot of vodka.

10 Bellevue
MAP M2 ■ Kempinski Hotel, Nab. Reki Moyki 22 ■ 335 9111 ■ ₽₽

Located in the Kempinski Hotel, Bellevue offers fine European-style food and a fantastic view of the city from its wall-to-wall glass windows.

→ See map on pp72–3

Bars and Cafés

The quirky Republic of Cats

1 Republic of Cats
MAP B4 ◼ Ulitsa Yakubovicha 10 ◼ 312 0487 ◼ ₽

Have tea with a tabby cat at this café, which lets you socialize with the cats while supporting a local shelter.

2 Café Zoom
MAP L4 ◼ Gorokhovaya ulitsa 22 ◼ 612 1329 ◼ ₽

Young art professionals and students from the nearby design academy come here to linger over a coffee or to enjoy a quick, tasty meal.

3 The Office Pub
MAP M4 ◼ Kazanskaya ulitsa 5 ◼ 571 5428 ◼ ₽

An Irish bar serving Guinness, along with a huge selection of beers and whiskies. Popular with expats, tourists and locals, it's a buzzing place with an upbeat atmosphere.

4 Teplo
MAP K4 ◼ Bolshaya Morskaya ulitsa 45 ◼ 570 1974 ◼ ₽

Meaning "warm" in Russian, Teplo is cosy and welcoming, with alfresco dining throughout the summer. On the menu are Russian favourites alongside Italian classics.

5 Astra
MAP J3 ◼ Admiralteyskaya nab. 2 ◼ 320 0877 ◼ ₽

One of the attractive boat restaurants, Astra serves European and Russian food, as it is moored on the River Neva.

6 Baraka
MAP M3 ◼ Kazanskaya ulitsa 10 ◼ 904 7077 ◼ ₽

This café offers fresh vegetarian Indian, vegan Moroccan and European cuisine, delicious desserts and superb drinks.

7 Terrassa
MAP M3 ◼ Kazanskaya ulitsa 3 ◼ 640 1616 ◼ ₽₽

Boasting fabulous panoramic views across the city, this is the ideal place for a special meal in fine weather.

8 Shatush
MAP L4 ◼ Nab. Reki Moyki 64 ◼ 914 4343 ◼ ₽

An elegant restaurant specializing in eastern food, including a fine selection of Japanese and Arabic dishes.

9 Barbaris
MAP J4 ◼ Pochtamtskiy pereulok 8 ◼ 312 0343 ◼ ₽

This café offers delectable European and Oriental cuisine. The *shashlyk* (shish kebab) and baklava are particularly recommended.

10 HI SO Terrace
MAP K3 ◼ Voznesenskiy prospekt 6 ◼ 610 6161

The glamorous Hi So Terrace hosts a sophisticated crowd. Enjoy a cocktail and admire the spectacular views from the terrace in the warmer months.

Panoramic views from HI SO Terrace

TOP 10 Sennaya Ploshchad

One of St Petersburg's oldest residential areas, Sennaya ploshchad was a hotbed of poverty, crime and filth in the 19th century. Dostoevsky found the subject matter for many of his novels in these streets. An area of sharp contrasts, it is home to both crumbling, century-old houses and palatial residences. The area has much to offer, including the world-famous Mariinskiy Theatre and stunning St Nicholas's Cathedral. Streets twist artfully around the Griboedov Canal, the Moyka and the Fontanka.

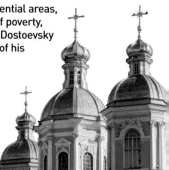

Gilded domes of St Nicholas's Cathedral

SENNAYA PLOSHCHAD

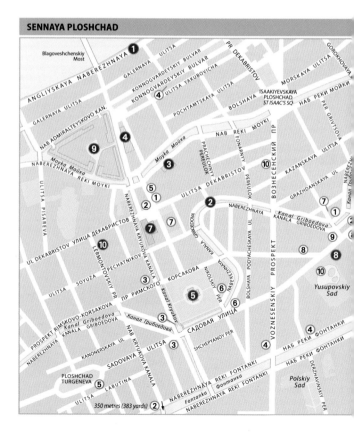

350 metres (383 yards)

1 The English Quay
MAP J3 ■ Angliyskaya nab.

This collection of buildings gets its name from the English merchants who settled here in the 1730s. They turned the area into a little slice of England and influenced, among other things, the development of football in the city. The mansion at No. 10 featured in Tolstoy's novel *War and Peace*, and No. 28 was once the headquarters of the Socialist Revolutionary Party.

2 The Lion Bridge
MAP J5 ■ Lviniy most

The Lion Bridge, with its elegant, cast-iron lions that hold up the bridge's supports, is a favourite place for couples of all ages to meet

Cast-iron lions of the Lion Bridge

before heading off to walk along the atmospheric Griboedov Canal. Dating from the early 19th century, this bridge is a jewel in the heart of Sennaya ploshchad, and one of the city's most recognized landmarks.

3 Yusupov Palace
MAP J5 ■ Nab. Reki Moyki 94 ■ 314 9883 ■ Open 11am–5pm ■ Adm

Purchased by the wealthy, aristocratic Yusupov family in 1830 to house their personal art collection, the yellow colonnaded Yusupov Palace was designed by Vallin de la Mothe in the 1860s. Its interior is notable for the exotic Moorish Room, with its Islamic-influenced mosaics, arches and fountains. The palace takes its place in history due to the murder of Rasputin *(see p80)* here in the winter of 1916. The cellar houses an exhibition dedicated to him.

Moorish Room in the Yusupov Palace

4 Central Naval Museum

MAP B5 ▪ Ploshchad Truda ▪ 303 8513 ▪ Open 11am–6pm Wed–Sun ▪ Adm ▪ www.navalmuseum.ru

One of the world's largest naval museums has more than 800 exhibits telling the fascinating story of the Russian navy. Intricate shipbuilding models form the core of the collection, and can be traced back to the time of Peter the Great and his grand vision of a Russian navy – the museum's prize exhibit is the small boat with which he first learnt to sail as a boy, inspiring his fascination with the sea.

RASPUTIN

Rasputin was a Russian peasant mystic who, after "miraculously" curing Nicholas II's son of haemophilia, came to exercise considerable, and not entirely benign, influence over the Russian court. On 17 December 1916, a group of nobles, fearful of the control he exerted, set upon him at Yusupov Palace. Poisoned, shot and clubbed, he succumbed to death, his frozen body recovered from the Neva three days later.

Dome of St Nicholas's Cathedral

5 St Nicholas's Cathedral

MAP J6 ▪ Nikolskaya ploshchad ▪ 714 7085 ▪ Open 6am–7:30pm

Overlooking Kryukov Canal, St Nicholas's Cathedral, with its striking sky-blue and white Baroque façade, appears out of place in the seedy and crumbling streets of Sennaya ploshchad. Completed in 1762, the cathedral was originally intended for sailors and employees of the nearby Admiralty (see p73), and was known for years by residents as the "Sailors' Church". It contains a collection of rare 18th-century icons.

6 Sennaya Ploshchad

MAP L5

At the heart of the district to which it gives its name is one of the city's oldest squares. Sennaya ploshchad has long had a reputation for poverty and crime. In the 18th century, it was home to the city's cheapest and rowdiest street markets. Soviet authorities attempted to clean up the area, closing down the market and renaming the square "Ploshchad Mira" ("Peace Square"). Today, it houses several shopping malls, as well as an intersection to three central metro stations.

7 Mariinskiy Theatre

The dazzling Mariinskiy Theatre (see pp20–21), also known as the Kirov, has witnessed performances by a number of Russia's most illustrious ballet dancers over the years, including legends such as Nureyev and Nijinsky. Located in Theatre Square, all visitors to the city should aim to see a performance here – it is a chance to experience a Russian

Performance at the Mariinskiy Theatre

occasion that remains essentially unchanged since the country's pre-revolutionary days.

⑧ Railway Museum
MAP L6 ■ Sadovaya ulitsa 50 ■ 315 1476 ■ Open 11am–5pm Sun–Thu ■ Adm ■ www.cmzt.narod.ru

A museum with exhibits that will interest history buffs of all ages, including a fascinating display on aspects of luxury travel in the tsarist era. The museum was established in 1913, and has over 50,000 items on display, which date from pre-revolutionary Russian carriages to present-day engines.

Exhibit at the Railway Museum

⑨ New Holland
MAP B5 ■ Nab. Reki Moyki ■ Open 9am–10pm Mon–Thu (to 11pm Fri–Sun)

This triangular island gets its name from the Dutch craftsmen that assisted Peter the Great in building the country's first navy. Constructed in 1719 to store timber for the building of ships, the island has been transformed into a cultural centre. It hosts concerts and features cafes, restaurants, a play-ground, a beach during summer as well as a skating rink in winters.

⑩ Choral Synagogue
MAP B5 ■ Lermontovskiy prospekt 2 ■ 713 8186 ■ Open 9:30am–6pm

Opened in 1893, this synagogue was the result of the Jewish community's rebirth after years of repression during the reign of Nicholas I. Designed by Ivan Shaposhnikov in Moorish style, its cupola is almost 47 m (154 ft) high.

A STROLL BEFORE A SHOW

▶ AFTERNOON

In order to attend an evening performance at the legendary **Mariinskiy Theatre** (see pp20–21), begin your walk at 4pm. Starting at the bustling square, Sennaya ploshchad, head across the road outside the exit to Sadovaya Metro station, and walk in the direction of the nab. Kanala Griboedova. Turn left and follow the canal away from the metro towards the 19th-century **Lion Bridge** (see p79), being sure to pay close attention to the magnificently sculpted lions. Cross the bridge, then take a right onto Ulitsa Dekabristov, followed by a left into the narrow Prachechnyy pereulok; continue down the street to its very end, turning left at the Moyka. Ahead of you is the yellow façade of **Yusupov Palace** (see p79). Audio guides are available in English and many other languages. Don't forget to check out the exhibition in the basement devoted to the infamous Rasputin.

EVENING

After Yusupov Palace, follow the Moyka down to Potseluev most (Bridge of Kisses) and take the first left. Ahead of you is **St Nicholas's Cathedral**. After exploring its opulent interior, retrace your steps back along Ulitsa Glinki, named after the 19th-century Russian composer, Mikhail Glinka. It should now be time to take your seats at the Mariinskiy Theatre. After the performance has ended, relax over a filling meal at nearby Sadko restaurant (see p83).

See map on pp78–9 ←

The Best of the Rest

1 Rim
MAP L5 ■ Nab. Kanala
Griboedova 69 ■ 314 1222 ■ ₽
Delicious Italian dishes, a good choice
of wines and friendly staff await you
at this restaurant and bar located in
an 1828 building where renowned
writer Nikolai Gogol lived for a while.

2 People-Watching in Sennaya Ploshchad
MAP L5
Day or night, Sennaya ploshchad
is a hive of activity. Grab a beer and
a pie from a street stall and indulge
in some people-watching.

3 Seven Bridges
MAP B6 ■ Pikalov Bridge,
Kanal Griboedova 131
One of the most beautiful spots in
the city that offers a spectacular
view of at least seven local bridges
set at the confluence of canals.

4 Marina Gisich Gallery
MAP C5 ■ Nab. Reki Fontanki
121 ■ 314 4380
One of the city's premier private
galleries of contemporary art is
housed in this fantastic converted flat.

5 Dva-Mu
MAP B6 ■ Sadovaya ulitsa 94
■ 714 5084 ■ ₽
Named after a popular Russian
children's story, self-service
Dva-Mu serves inexpensive yet
healthy Russian fast food.

6 Entrée
MAP J6 ■ Nikolskaya
ploshchad 6 ■ 572 5201 ■ ₽
Serving an excellent standard of
French-European cuisine, Entrée
is a chic choice for diners attending
performances at the Mariinskiy
Theatre. Service is superlative and
there is an exceptional wine list.

7 Rimsky-Korsakov Conservatory
MAP J5 ■ Teatralnaya ploshchad 3
■ 312 2519 ■ Performances 7pm
■ Adm ■ www.conservatory.ru
Russia's oldest music school
was founded in 1862 by Anton
Rubinstein. Notable alumni
include Pyotr Tchaikovsky, Sergei
Prokofiev and, in the Soviet period,
Dmitri Shostakovich.

8 Sennaya Market
MAP L5 ■ Moskovskiy
prospekt 4 ■ 310 1209
One of the oldest markets in the
city, this is a great place to explore
even if you don't buy anything.

9 Kroshka-Kartoshka
MAP L5 ■ Moskovskiy
prospekt 2
Part of a chain of food stands that offer
baked potatoes with a range of fillings.

10 Yusupov Garden
MAP L6 ■ Sadovaya ulitsa 54
Take a break from the crowds with
a stroll in this romantic park.

The lake in Yusupov Garden

Restaurants

Pretty interior at Sadko

5 Teatro
MAP J5 ■ Ulitsa Glinki 2
■ 900 4488 ■ ₽

This spacious and elegant restaurant serves a wide selection of seafood and Russian dishes.

6 Izba
MAP K6 ■ Sadovaya ulitsa 67
■ 310 6194 ■ ₽

Izba (which means country cottage) is the perfect spot to sample some authentic Russian dishes in a traditional setting.

7 Severyanin
MAP L5 ■ Stolyarnyy pereulok 18 ■ 951 6396 ■ ₽₽

Run by celebrity chef Aram Mnatsakanov, Severyanin has a classic 19th-century interior and specializes in traditional north Russian cuisine.

1 Sadko
MAP J5 ■ Ulitsa Glinki 2
■ 903 2373 ■ ₽

Sadko is an ideal place for a meal after watching a performance at the nearby Mariinskiy Theatre.

2 Khochu Kharcho
MAP L5 ■ Sadovaya ulitsa 39/41 ■ 310 3236 ■ ₽

Georgian dishes form the basis of the extensive menu. There's also a fantastic sommelier.

3 Romeo's Bar and Kitchen
MAP B5 ■ Prospekt Rimskovo-Korsakova 43
■ 572 5448 ■ ₽

A popular choice for theatre-goers, with a superb menu of Russian and Italian dishes.

Berry tarts at Romeo's Bar and Kitchen

8 Meatarea Chuck
MAP M5 ■ Gorokhovaya ulitsa 41 ■ 584 9394 ■ ₽

This trendy restaurant has graffitied raw concrete walls and offers hearty meals served on wooden chopping boards.

9 Toscana Grill
MAP L6
■ Sadovaya ulitsa 47
■ 245 3217 ■ ₽

A good central option featuring Italian grilled meats and pizza dishes.

4 Russian Vodka Room No. 1
MAP B4 ■ Konnogvardeyskiy bulvar 4 ■ 570 6420 ■ ₽₽

Enjoy the selection of Russian vodkas along with traditional cuisine (see p59).

10 1913
MAP K5 ■ Voznesenskiy prospekt 13/2 ■ 315 5148 ■ ₽₽

This traditional restaurant provides live music and regional fare made with locally sourced ingredients.

See map on pp78–9

Bars

① Vsekhorosho
MAP M5 ■ Sadovaya ulitsa 27 ■ 424 3838

This democratic style restaurant offers European and Asian cuisine. The theme parties hosted here change the atmosphere with lively dancing.

② Shamrock
MAP B5 ■ Ulitsa Dekabristov 27 ■ 570 4625

A local institution, Shamrock has live music most days of the week (except on Tue and Fri). You may even spot a prima ballerina from the nearby Mariinskiy Theatre (see pp20–21).

③ Pyshechnaya
MAP N2 ■ Sadovaya ulitsa 32 ■ 310 5239

This tiny stand-up coffee bar offers only hot coffee and sugar-coated doughnuts. Join the lengthy queues for a taste of Soviet nostalgia.

④ Tequila Boom
MAP B5 ■ Voznesenskiy prospekt 57 ■ 310 1534

This Mexican bar-restaurant holds popular theme nights, which usually involve customers downing large quantities of tequila.

Mexican-themed Tequila Boom

⑤ Dickens
MAP C5 ■ Nab. Reki Fontanki 108 ■ 702 6263

This English-style bar has an excellent beer and whisky selection and serves great food, including breakfast, in the restaurant on the first floor.

Interior of Jager

⑥ Jager
MAP M5 ■ Gorokhovaya ulitsa 34 ■ 310 8270

With local and imported beer on tap, hearty German food and live accordion music, this small corner of Bavaria in the heart of the city is always busy.

⑦ Pif Paf Bar
MAP C4 ■ Nab. Kanala Griboedova 31 ■ 312 6227

With a café and an on-site barber shop, hip Pif Paf is one of the city's most popular cocktail and burger bars.

⑧ SPB
MAP L5 ■ Sadovaya ulitsa 42a ■ 655 6708

Crowds of students gather at this popular beer hall, which serves local and international brews and turns out decent pub fare.

⑨ Hugs Bar
MAP M4 ■ Nab.Kanala Griboedova 38/1 ■ 923 5555

Catch performances by cover groups, and enjoy the jazz concerts at this friendly bar. The menu offers European cuisine and craft beer.

⑩ Wave Burgers&More
MAP M5 ■ Nab. Kanala Griboedova 38/1 ■ 997 2849 ■ www.wave-burgers.com

The city's best spot for craft beer and high-quality burgers, with classic beef, vegan and crabmeat options.

See map on pp78–9

Clubs and Nightspots

1 **Laboratory 31**
MAP M4 ▪ Gorokhovaya ulitsa 31 ▪ 737 3577 ▪ Open 3pm–6am
This unusual bar with neon lighting has a laboratory theme. The cocktails, named after chemicals, are served in steaming test-tubes.

2 **Sky Bar**
MAP B6 ▪ Lermontovskiy pr. 43/1 ▪ 740 2999 ▪ Open 5pm–2am
On the 18th floor of the Azimut Hotel, this cocktail bar is well worth a visit for its outstanding city views.

3 **Old Dogs**
MAP B6 ▪ Sadovaya ulitsa 66 ▪ 572 5700 ▪ Open midday–3am
This welcoming Irish bar has a great selection of beers and whiskies, good music and a menu of hearty meat-based dishes. Friday and Saturday nights are especially lively.

4 **Central Station**
MAP M4 ▪ Lomonosova ulitsa 1 ▪ 312 3600 ▪ Open 10pm–6am ▪ Adm
The city's largest gay club is usually packed with an international crowd enjoying drag shows and karaoke.

5 **More Chaya**
MAP M5 ▪ Nab. Reki Fontanki 91 ▪ 310 3698 ▪ Open 10am–10pm ▪ Adm for tea ceremonies
Located on the bank of the Fontanka river, this unusual club holds tea ceremonies and sells high-quality Chinese tea. Call ahead for bookings.

6 **Bermudy**
MAP M4 ▪ Bankovskiy pereulok 6 ▪ 325 5550 ▪ Open 6pm–2am Sun–Thu, 8pm–6am Fri & Sat
This small, cheerful bar with a young crowd turns into a disco after midnight.

7 **Money Honey**
MAP M5 ▪ Sadovaya ulitsa 28–30, Apraksin dvor, bld 13 ▪ 310 0549 ▪ Open 10am–6am ▪ Adm for some events
Cheap beer and dancing draw the student population to this Western-saloon-style venue.

8 **Gallery Bar**
MAP C5 ▪ Ambassador Hotel, Prospekt Rimskovo-Korsakova 5–7 ▪ 609 0992 ▪ Open daily
With great city views, this is a sophisticated spot with regular exhibitions of contemporary art.

9 **Ruki Vverh**
MAP M4 ▪ Nab. Kanala Griboedova 28 ▪ 416 4390 ▪ Open 6pm–6am
This club features nostalgic music and 1990s interiors. There is a karaoke restaurant too.

10 **Manhattan**
MAP N5 ▪ Nab. Reki Fontanki 90 ▪ 713 1945 ▪ Open noon–6am ▪ Adm
This live music club has a great atmosphere and a cheap bar.

The stage at popular club Manhattan

ⓉⓄⓅ⑩ Vasilevskiy Island

Peter the Great originally intended Vasilevskiy Island, the largest island in St Petersburg, to be the administrative centre of his "Window to Europe", but constant flooding and the hazards of crossing the Neva caused him to change his mind. However, the island was not forgotten. Its lower-eastern area, known locally as the Strelka, or Spit, is home to a cluster of fascinating sights, including a pair of eye-catching 15th-century BC sphinxes, the city's first museum and the grand, russet-coloured, 19th-century Rostral Columns, originally oil-lit lighthouses. Vasilevskiy Island is a splendid, detached area of St Petersburg and, with its wide, tree-lined avenues, it has an exceedingly calm atmosphere.

A 15th-century sphinx on Vasilevskiy Island

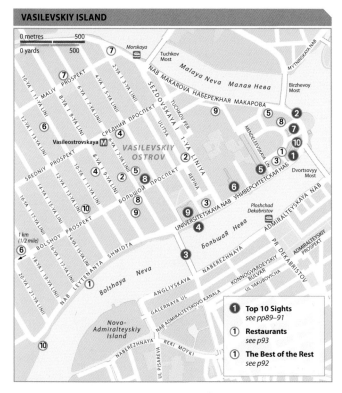

VASILEVSKIY ISLAND

Top 10 Sights
see pp89–91

Restaurants
see p93

The Best of the Rest
see p92

Previous pages *The frescoed interior of the Church on Spilled Blood*

Blagoveshchenskiy Bridge over the river Neva

① Kunstkammer
MAP K2 ■ Universitetskaya nab. 3 ■ 328 1412 ■ Open 11am–6pm Tue–Sun (closed last Tue of month) ■ Adm ■ www.kunstkamera.ru

While the Kunstkammer is notorious for Peter the Great's bizarre collection of deformed foetuses, the museum is also home to an exhaustive Soviet-era exhibition on "The Peoples of the World" – an old-fashioned but informative display of artifacts and comical waxworks. In the main part of the museum, look out for the heart and skeleton of Peter the Great's personal servant, a 2.27-m (7.5-ft) giant, and a display of teeth pulled out by the tsar, who boasted dentistry as his hobby.

② Rostral Columns
MAP C3 ■ Birzhevaya ploshchad

Flanking the former St Petersburg Stock Exchange (see p90), the imposing Rostral Columns (1810) were designed as lighthouses by Thomas de Thomon. The enormous figures at the bases of the two columns represent four of the country's biggest rivers – the Neva, Volga, Dnieper and Volkhov. The columns are decorated in Roman style with ships' prows jutting out from each side. Their gas torches are still lit on special occasions.

A Rostral Column

③ Blagoveshchenskiy Bridge
MAP B4

Having gone through numerous name changes and reconstructions since it was built in 1850, this bridge marks the border between the river Neva and the Gulf of Finland. When built it was the longest bridge in Europe; Nicholas I promoted the architect for each completed span.

④ Sphinxes
MAP B4

This pair of 15th-century BC sphinxes was discovered in Thebes in ancient Egypt in the mid-19th century and later brought to St Petersburg. A local landmark, the sphinxes' faces are said to resemble Pharaoh Amenhotep II.

⑤ Twelve Colleges
MAP J2
■ Universitetskaya nab. 7
■ Closed to public

This Baroque edifice, built between 1722 and 1742, was originally intended to house Russia's 12 government bodies. In 1835 the building was given to St Petersburg University. Famous former students here include Lenin and eight Nobel Prize winners. Just outside stands a bronze statue of Russia's premier Enlightenment scientist, Mikhail Lomonosov (1711–65).

The elegant interior of Menshikov Palace

6 Menshikov Palace
MAP B3 ▪ Universitetskaya
nab. 15 ▪ 323 1112 ▪ Open 10:30am–
6pm Tue, Thu, Sat & Sun (to 9pm Wed
& Fri) ▪ Adm

This Baroque palace (1720) was one
of the first stone buildings in the city.
Now a branch of the Hermitage *(see
pp14–17)*, it houses an exhibition on
18th-century Russian culture which
features the opulent rooms of Prince
Menshikov (1673–1729), who was later
exiled to Siberia for treason. While
living here, Menshikov regularly
entertained and once organized a
"dwarf wedding" for Peter the Great.

7 Old Stock Exchange
MAP B3 ▪ Birzhevaya
ploshchad 4 ▪ Closed to public

With its sculpture of Neptune being
drawn in a chariot by sea horses, the
Old Stock Exchange was modelled
on a famous Greek temple at
Paestum in Italy. The building was
transformed in 1940 and housed
the naval museum until 2012. The
Russian government now has plans
to turn the impressive structure
into a Federal courthouse.

8 St Andrew's Cathedral
MAP A3 ▪ 6-ya Liniya 11
▪ 323 3418 ▪ Open 9am–9pm

The highlight of St Andrew's
Cathedral is its 18th-century
iconostasis, which includes some
extremely rare icons. It stands on
the site of a smaller, wooden church,
which was destroyed in 1761 after
being struck by lightning. During
the World War II siege of the city
(see p38), the church's dome
housed artillery units.

9 Academy of Arts
MAP B4 ▪ Universitetskaya
nab. 17 ▪ 323 3578 ▪ Open
11am–7pm Wed–Sun ▪ Adm
▪ www.nimrah.ru

The Neo-Classical Academy of
Arts (1788) was the birthplace
of the Russian Realist art movement,
whose founders became known as
The Wanderers. The group formed in
1863, when 14 discontented students

Old Stock Exchange

STALINISM

Joseph Stalin (1878–1953) became leader of the Soviet Union in 1922. The dictator led the country through World War II and transformed it into a global superpower. From 1930 onwards, he instigated the "Great Terror" – millions were exiled to labour camps, some never to return. After his death, new Soviet leader Nikita Khrushchev began the process of de-Stalinization.

walked out of their exams in protest against the strict conservatism of their lecturers. The academy's students included painter Ilya Repin, and architects Andrey Zakharov and Andrey Voronikhin. Look out for the conference hall's magnificent ceiling painting by Vasiliy Shebuev.

Display at the Zoological Museum

10 Zoological Museum

MAP B3 ■ Universitetskaya nab. 1/3 ■ 328 0112 ■ Open 11am–6pm Wed–Mon (closed every second Wed) ■ Adm ■ www.zin.ru/museum

Founded by Peter the Great, this museum presents one of the biggest collections of stuffed animals in the world. It contains part of his taxidermic collection, including a horse that the tsar once rode into battle. The museum is also renowned for its stunning collection of mammoths.

A WALK AROUND THE STRELKA

▶ MORNING

All the main sights on Vasilevskiy Island are relatively close, so there is no need for public transport or excruciatingly long walks. Start the morning at the 19th-century **Rostral Columns** (see p89), admiring the view across the Neva. Perhaps St Petersburg's defining feature is the river, which lies frozen in winter. Afterwards, cross over the road to Universitetskaya nab. and walk down to the city's oldest museum, the **Kunstkammer** (see p89). Spend some time exploring Peter the Great's mania for biological oddities. When you have sufficiently recovered, walk the short distance towards the **Academy of Arts**, home of the Russian Realist art movement. Directly across the road from the Academy are the **Sphinxes** (see p89), standing guard on the riverside. The sphinxes are a popular meeting point for the city's youth. Buy a memento from the numerous souvenir sellers here, and then stroll towards the expansive **Blagoveshchenskiy Bridge** (see p89), which was extensively renovated in 2007.

AFTERNOON

Now walk down to the splendid 18th-century **St Andrew's Cathedral**, and admire its breathtaking collection of icons. Afterwards, go back to Universitetskaya nab. and drop in at **Pryanosti i Radosti** (see p93), housed in No.13 – one of the most beautiful buildings of Vasilevskiy Island. It was built by Domenico Tresini in the 18th century.

See map on p88 ←

The Best of the Rest

C-189 Submarine Museum

MAP A4 ▪ Nab. Leytenanta Shmidta, 16 liniya ▪ 613 7099 ▪ Open 11am–7pm Wed–Sun ▪ Adm

Launched in 1954, this 76-m (249-ft) diesel attack submarine served in the Soviet navy until 1990. Visitors can explore its cramped interior and operate the periscope.

2 St Catherine Church

MAP B3 ▪ Bolshoy prospekt 1 ▪ 323 1852 ▪ Adm

Weekly Sunday concerts of classical music as well as religious services are held at this 18th-century church.

3 Rumyantsevskiy Garden

MAP B4 ▪ Universitetskaya nab. 15/17

One of the oldest gardens in the city hosts concerts on Sundays during the warmer months.

4 Red Cube

MAP A3 ▪ Sredniy prospekt 26/28 ▪ 8 (800) 200 8009

Red Cube, a fashionable shop selling items such as clocks, mugs and ornaments, is good for gift-shopping.

5 The Institute of Russian Literature (Pushkin House)

MAP J1 ▪ Naberzhnaya Makarova 4 ▪ 328 1901

This museum houses manuscripts and exhibits relating to Russia's greatest poet, as well as to other eminent writers such as Gogol, Tolstoy, Turgenev and Dostoevsky.

Exhibits at Erarta Museum

6 Erarta Museum

29-ya liniya 2 ▪ 324 0809 ▪ Open 10am–10pm Wed–Mon ▪ Adm

One of Russia's largest private museums of contemporary art showcases emerging and established Russian artists.

7 Wild Duck Pub

MAP A2 ▪ 7-ya liniya 72/17 ▪ 323 8088

Irish pub Wild Duck offers live music and a massive selection of beers.

8 Casa Del Myaso

MAP K2 ▪ Birzhevoy proezd 6 ▪ 320 9746 ▪ ₽₽

Carnivores need look no further. This restaurant is devoted to the glories of meat in all its variety, including game.

9 8th Line Pub

MAP A4 ▪ Sokos Hotel Vasilievsky, 8-ya liniya 11–13 ▪ 335 2290

This Finnish take on a traditional English pub provides a tranquil spot for an evening's relaxation, or a quick stop for traditional English pub food.

10 Icebreaker Krasin

Nab. Leytenanta Shmidta, 23 liniya ▪ 325 35 47 ▪ Open Wed–Sun, tours hourly 11am–5pm ▪ Adm ▪ www.krassin.ru

Krasin was the world's most powerful icebreaker ship from the time of its construction in 1917 until the mid-1950s. Visitors can step on board and discover its history, including several daring arctic rescues.

The Institute of Russian Literature

Restaurants

1 Staraya Tamozhnya
MAP B4 ■ Tamozhennyy pereulok 1 ■ 327 8980 ■ ₽₽

Drop in here after a visit to the Kunstkammer (see p89), if Peter the Great's weird collections haven't spoilt your appetite. The menu is strongly based around French cuisine and the interiors are traditional.

2 Ukrop Kvartira Café
MAP A ■ 37-ya liniya 30 ■ 946 3003 ■ ₽

This café serves delicious vegetarian food in an eco-friendly interior and at reasonable prices.

3 Restoran
MAP B3 ■ Tamozhennyy pereulok 2 ■ 327 8979 ■ ₽

Classic Russian dishes are served alongside a tempting selection of infused vodkas.

4 Café Abajour
MAP A3 ■ 9-ya liniya 30 ■ 409 0039 ■ ₽

The superb menu at this café features classic Russian dishes with a modern twist, such as duck and blue-cheese salad.

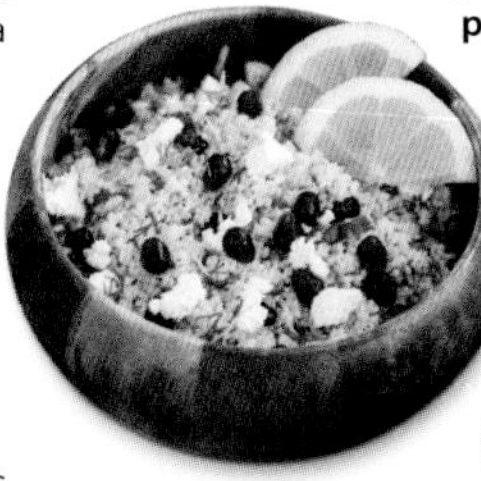

A colourful bowl of couscous salad

5 Pryanosti i Radosti
MAP B3 ■ 6-ya liniya 13 ■ 640 1616 ■ ₽

This place offers cuisine from Asia, Europe and the Caucasus. Spread over multiple halls, the modern, colourful interior is comfortable and warm. The restaurant also has a children's area with a huge ship.

6 La Botanique
MAP A3 ■ 11-ya liniya 50 ■ 323 2231 ■ ₽

Presentation is key at this bright and airy hotel-restaurant, which offers international fare in a relaxed environment. There is also a well-chosen wine list.

7 Pierrot
MAP A2 ■ 2-ya liniya 61/30a ■ 438 5622 ■ ₽

Catering mainly to a business clientele, this restaurant on the water's edge serves French and Russian dishes in a minimal and stylish setting.

8 Grolle Tavern
MAP A4 ■ Bolshoy prospekt 20 ■ 323 6258 ■ ₽

The varied live music and fresh fish dishes make this maritime-themed tavern a great place to stop for a drink and a meal.

9 Dans le Noir
MAP B3 ■ Sokos Hotel, Birzhevoi pereulok 2-4 ■ 335 2212 ■ ₽₽

Dine in total darkness to heighten your senses as you taste, smell and touch the food. Blind waiters serve a choice of four specially designed surprise menus, the contents of which are revealed after your meal.

10 Sakartvelo
MAP A4 ■ 12-ya liniya 13 ■ 947 7878 ■ ₽

This boisterous family-owned Georgian restaurant serves large portions of home-cooked food at reasonable prices. Meals may be accompanied by live Georgian music and dance performed by the owners.

See map on p88 ←

TOP 10 Petrogradskaya

Manchurian Lion

Although the founding of the city dates from the construction of the Peter and Paul Fortress, Petrogradskaya was sparsely populated until the building of Trinity Bridge in 1903, when the area became accessible from the centre of the city. It quickly became one of the city's most popular spots. During the ensuing building boom, many Style-Moderne buildings were commissioned, a trend which helped to shape the area's present-day character and atmosphere. While the Peter and Paul Fortress is the main tourist highlight, Petrogradskaya, with its iconic Cruiser *Aurora* and exotic Sobornaya Mosque, is rich in cultural and architectural delights. From the desolate swampland where Peter the Great chose to found his city to today's elegant, residential area, Petrogradskaya has come a long way.

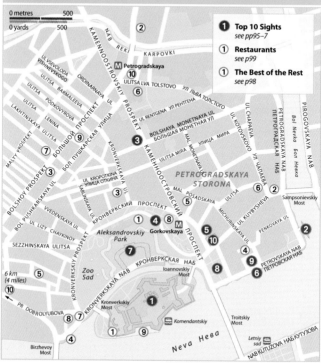

PETROGRADSKAYA

1 **Top 10 Sights**
see pp95–7

1 **Restaurants**
see p99

1 **The Best of the Rest**
see p98

Cathedral of SS Peter and Paul

① Peter and Paul Fortress

This fortress (see pp24–5) is where Peter the Great once strolled, dreaming of the city to come; where Dostoevsky (see p46) was imprisoned for his political beliefs; and where Nicholas II (see p39) was laid to rest decades after his execution. The Baroque Cathedral of SS Peter and Paul here forms a magnificent setting for the tombs of the Romanov monarchs.

② Cruiser Aurora

MAP D2 ■ Petrogradskaya nab. 4 ■ 607 4922 ■ Open 11am–6pm Wed–Sun ■ Adm ■ www.eng.navalmuseum.ru

On 25 October 1917 at 9:40pm, the cruiser *Aurora* gave the signal for the storming of the Winter Palace by firing a blank round from the bow gun. At the beginning of the siege of the city (see p38), the ship was sunk to protect it from the Nazis. Raised from the depths in 1944, the *Aurora* was turned into a museum in 1956.

③ Kirov Museum

MAP C1 ■ Kamennoostrovskiy prospekt 26–28 ■ 346 0217 ■ Open 11am–6pm Thu–Tue ■ Adm ■ www.kirovmuseum.ru

The downfall of the Soviet politician Sergey Kirov was his popularity, for which Stalin is thought to have had him murdered in 1934. This event sparked the Great Terror of the 1930s, during which executions became a fact of life (see p39). Kirov's flat, which houses the museum, has been preserved as it was during his lifetime, and contains documents and photographs chronicling his political career.

④ Aleksandrovskiy Park

MAP C2

The one-time cultural centre of the Petrogradskaya area, this park was home to varying forms of entertainment during the 20th century, including performances in the Opera House (1911) and clown and animal acts in the People's House, which was founded by Nicholas II in 1900. The park still draws crowds today. It is home to the zoo, the planetarium and the Music Hall, formerly the Opera House, which hosts pop concerts.

⑤ Sobornaya Mosque

MAP C2 ■ Kamennoostrovskiy prospekt 7 ■ 233 9819 ■ Open 10am–5pm ■ Book in advance

One of Europe's largest mosques, Sobornaya Mosque can hold up to 5,000 people. Constructed in 1913 by Nikolai Vasiliev and Stepan Krichinskiy with money collected by Russian Muslims, it has a sky-blue cupola and minarets, and a grey granite exterior. Used as a warehouse during much of the Soviet period, the mosque is back in service today. Access is limited for non-Muslims, but is possible outside prayer times.

Exterior of the Sobornaya Mosque

6 Manchurian Lions
MAP D2 ■ Petrovskaya nab. 6

This pair of unusual frog-lions, which stand opposite the cabin of Peter the Great on the water's edge, were brought from the Manchurian town of Gurin during the Russo-Japanese War of 1904–5. A local landmark, they were presented to the city by General Grodekov in 1907, and are known in St Petersburg as the Shih Tzsa (Chinese for lion).

Tank at the Artillery Museum

7 Artillery Museum
MAP C2 ■ Aleksandrovskiy Park 7 ■ 232 0296 ■ Open 11am–6pm Wed–Sun; closed last Thu of month ■ Adm ■ www.artillery-museum.ru

Along with the Kunstkammer (see p89), this is one of St Petersburg's oldest museums, with plans for its foundation dating from the construction of the city in 1703. Built between 1849 and 1860, the museum is housed in a horseshoe-shaped, red-brick building designed by the Russian architect Pyotr Tamanskiy. It contains

ISLAM IN RUSSIA

Russia is a great deal more multi-ethnic and multi-religious than many people think. The Sobornaya Mosque acts as a meeting place for believers from Russia's mostly Muslim Caucasus region, home to Dagestan and Chechnya, where war has raged since 1991. Relations between Muslims and Slavic Russians are tense.

hundreds of weapons, many of them dating back to medieval times; most of the exhibitions are connected in some way with Russia's victorious 1812 war against Napoleon.

8 Trinity Square
MAP D2 ■ Troitskaya ploshchad

Known as Revolution Square during the Soviet era (see p42), this square owes its name to the Church of the Trinity that once stood here. Built in 1710 and destroyed in the 1930s during the USSR's anti-religion campaign, the church served the area's merchants. Stretching from the square, across the widest point of the Neva river, is the elegant Trinity Bridge (see p40), a construction that transformed the area's fate by connecting it to the rest of the city.

Trinity Square

Cabin of Peter the Great

9 Cabin of Peter the Great

MAP D2 ▪ Petrovskaya nab. 6
▪ 232 4576 ▪ Open 10am–6pm Mon,
10am–6pm Wed, 1–9pm Thu, 10am–
6pm Fri–Sun; closed Tue ▪ Adm

Built from scratch in just three
days in May 1703, this was the city's
first building. Peter the Great, never
one for luxury, lived here for six
years, overseeing the construction
of his city. The brick walls were
added later by Catherine the Great.
A fascinating museum containing
some of Peter's personal posses-
sions, including his compass,
clothes and rowing boat, now
occupies the building.

10 Kshesinskaya Mansion

MAP D2 ▪ Ulitsa Kuybysheva 4
▪ 233 7052 ▪ Open 10am–6pm Sat–
Mon, 10am–8pm Wed & Fri; closed
last Mon of month ▪ Adm ▪ www.
polithistory.ru

This stylish mansion was once the
home of Matilda Kshesinskaya, a
ballerina at the Mariinskiy Theatre
(see pp20–21) during the late 19th century and lover of the future Nicholas II.
The mansion was designed for her
by the then court architect, Alexander
Von Gogen. The headquarters of the
Bolsheviks during the early days of
the 1917 Revolution, it now houses
the Museum of Russian Political
History (see p42).

A WALK THROUGH HISTORY

▶ MORNING

Start at Gorkovskaya metro
station and, crossing the road
via the underpass, walk down
Kamennoostrovskiy prospekt to
Sobornaya Mosque (see p95),
using its sky-blue minarets and
cupola to guide you – you may be
lucky enough to be allowed a look
inside. After that, walk down to
Trinity Square and admire the
elegant **Trinity Bridge** (see p40).
Without crossing the bridge,
turn left and take a stroll along
Petrovskaya nab., admiring the
views of the Neva. A short distance
from Trinity Bridge is the **Cabin of
Peter the Great**. Visit the museum
inside and, as you leave, don't
miss the **Manchurian Lions** on the
bank just opposite. Stop for lunch
at the **Volna (Wave)** (see p99).

AFTERNOON

After eating, stroll back to
Kamennoostrovskiy prospekt and
on to the **Peter and Paul Fortress**
(see pp24–5). A visit here will take
up the rest of the afternoon.
Be sure to see the magnificent
Cathedral of SS Peter and Paul
(see p24), seeking out the tombs
of the Romanov monarchs. A
visit to the **Trubetskoy Bastion**
(see p24), the home of countless
famous prisoners down the years,
is also not to be missed. If you
have time, stop by to observe
the controversial 1991 **Statue of
Peter the Great** (see p24) outside
Neva Gate, where prisoners were
exiled or sent off for execution.
Afterwards, if the weather is
good, head over to the beach
for a spot of sunbathing.

See map on p94

The Best of the Rest

1 ParkKing
MAP C2 ▪ Alexandrovskiy Park
4V (4B in Russian) ▪ 498 0606 ▪ Adm

A popular nightclub and restaurant, ParkKing attracts an energetic crowd with its dance and chill-out rooms.

Live performance at A2

2 A2
Prospekt Medikov 3 ▪ 333 0379 ▪ Adm

One of the city's most popular concert venues, A2 attracts top local and international acts, and is known for having the very best sound-system in town.

3 Mirage Cinema
MAP B1 ▪ Bolshoy prospekt 35
▪ 677 6060 ▪ Adm ▪ www.mirage.ru

With a sushi bar and gaming arcade, this stylish cinema is a great place to catch up on new releases.

4 Flying Dutchman
MAP B2 ▪ Mytinskaya nab. 6
▪ 313 8866/921 3676 ▪ PP

The Flying Dutchman, or *Letuchiy Gollandets*, is a club-restaurant that serves good beer. Its menu is an eclectic mix of world cuisines.

5 Kamchatka
MAP B2 ▪ Blohina ulitsa 15
▪ 7 921 987 2313 ▪ ₽

Located beneath a graffitied Soviet-era residential block, Kamchatka is a legendary underground rock club and museum, where beer drinking takes precedence over eating.

6 LabirintUm
MAP C1 ▪ Ulitsa Lva Tolstovo 9a
▪ 328 0008 ▪ Open 11am–7pm daily
▪ Adm ▪ www.labirint-um.ru

An interactive science museum that makes physics fun; perfect for kids overwhelmed by too much history.

7 Jean Jacques Rousseau
MAP B1 ▪ Gatchinskaya ulitsa
2/54 ▪ 232 9981 ▪ ₽

This French café boasts a long wine and spirits list. The delicious desserts make it a treat for Francophiles.

8 Mini St Petersburg
MAP C1 ▪ Aleksandrovskiy Park 5B

Stroll through Aleksandrovskiy Park *(see p95)* and enjoy seeing the city of St Petersburg in miniature, with all major landmarks represented.

9 The Riverbank
MAP C2 ▪ Petropavlovskaya Krepost

The beach just beyond the walls of the Peter and Paul Fortress *(see pp24–5)*, with its views of the Neva, is perfect for a lazy afternoon.

10 Saint Petersburg Stadium
MAP R2 ▪ Futbol'naya Alleya 1

Built in 2017, this stadium, also known as the Zenit Arena, is home to the city's top football team, Zenit *(see p55)*. It was also one of the venues for the 2018 FIFA World Cup.

Zenit's Alexander Kokorin in action

Restaurants

 Koryushka
MAP C2 ■ Petropavlovskaya
krepost 3 ■ 640 1616 ■ ₽₽

Set beside the Peter and Paul
Fortress, with sweeping views across
the Neva, Koryushka is part of the
Ginza chain and serves excellent
Georgian and Russian cuisine.

2 **Cherdak Attic**
MAP D1 ■ Ulitsa Kuybysheva
38/40 ■ 232 1182 ■ ₽

A cosy place for an evening meal,
Cherdak serves mainly European
dishes. Service is fast and friendly,
and the cocktails are excellent.

3 **Porter House**
MAP C2 ■ Voskova ulitsa
31/20 ■ 233 3352 ■ ₽

Choose from a vast range
of whiskies and imported
beers to pair with the
wide selection of con-
tinental cuisine.

4 **Volna (Wave)**
MAP D2
■ Petrovskaya nab. 4
■ 322 5383 ■ ₽

Volna is a fusion
restaurant that features
excellent fish dishes.
It also has a selection
of divine desserts.

5 **Flamand Rose**
MAP C1 ■ Malaya
Posadskaya ulitsa 7/4 ■ 498 5311 ■ ₽

Belgian classics and French
wine share menu space with
Russian favourites at this romantic restaurant that doubles up
as an antiques shop.

 Amazonki
MAP D1 ■ Ulitsa Chapaeva
4 ■ 232 9706 ■ ₽

European-style dishes are
served with salads that betray
hints of an Asian influence.
There is also a bamboo bar
serving great cocktails.

PRICE CATEGORIES
For a three-course meal for one with half
a bottle of wine, taxes and extra charges.

₽ under ₽4,000 ₽₽ ₽4,000–8,000
₽₽₽ over ₽8,000

 Mari Vanna
MAP B2 ■ Mytninskaya
Naberezhnaya 3 ■ 640 1616 ■ ₽₽

An authentic Russian restaurant with
a cosy interior, Mari Vanna provides a
good insight into the national cuisine.

8 **Probka**
MAP B2 ■ Dobrolyubova
prospekt 6 ■ 918 6910 ■ ₽₽

This highly regarded modern
restaurant is part of a chain run by
celebrity chef Aram Mnatsakanov.

The modern and chic interior of Probka

9 **Red Steak & Wine**
MAP B1 ■ Ulitsa Lenina 9
■ 927 4664 ■ ₽₽

Steaks cooked to order are
accompanied by a broad selection
of reasonably priced wines at this
popular steakhouse with a sleek
yet casual interior.

10 **Chekhov**
MAP C1 ■ Petropavlovskaya
ulitsa 4 ■ 234 4511 ■ ₽₽

Styled to resemble a 19th-century
cottage, this rustic restaurant is
renowned for its chicken Kiev.
Advance booking is recommended.

See map on p94

🔟 Further Afield

The outskirts of St Petersburg offer a lot in terms of architecture and historical monuments. The east of the city includes the Smolnyy Institute, which played a significant role in events immediately following the 1917 Revolution. To the north lies Finland Station and the train that brought Lenin home from exile in 1917. To the south is Moskovskaya ploshchad, the district Stalin attempted to make into the new city centre. On the city's far southern outskirts is the Neo-Gothic Chesma Church and the Victory Monument, a homage to the darkest days of World War II, dedicated to the siege victims.

Ornament at Tsarskoe Selo

FURTHER AFIELD

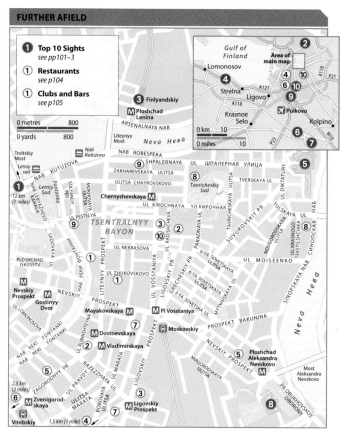

1 Top 10 Sights
see pp101–3

1 Restaurants
see p104

1 Clubs and Bars
see p105

The 87-storey Lakhta Center

1 Lakhta Center Tower
MAP Q1 ■ Lakhtinsky Prospekt 2 ■ www.lakhta.center

Standing at a height of 462 m (1,516 ft), the Lakhta Center is one of the tallest skyscrapers in Russia, as well as in Europe. Built on the coast of the Gulf of Finland, this business and cultural centre became fully operational in the fall of 2018. In addition to a two-level restaurant on the tower's 74th floor, outsiders can visit the planetarium as well as the sports and health centre.

2 Piskarevskoe Memorial Cemetery
MAP H1 ■ Prospekt Nepokorennykh 74 ■ 297 5716 ■ Memorial exhibition: Open 9am–6pm ■ www.pmemorial.ru

During the World War II siege (see p38) of the city, thousands of corpses were transported on sledges to cemeteries on the outskirts of town. Piskarevskoe was the largest of these, burying 420,000 people in 186 common graves. With an exhibition hall and a giant bronze statue of Mother Russia, the cemetery is a reminder of the horrors of war.

3 Finland Station
MAP E2 ■ Ploshchad Lenina 6

On 3 April 1917, the exiled Lenin and his Bolshevik companions returned from Switzerland to a triumphant reception at Finland Station. Forced again to flee the country for the summer, they returned in autumn, once more to Finland Station, and spurred the 1917 Revolution (see p38).

4 Peterhof
Of all St Petersburg's splendid royal estates, Peterhof (see pp30–31) is by far the most elegant. It is best visited between May and October, when the famous fountains are working and all the buildings are open to the public, but bear in mind that during this period it is at its most crowded. Inspired by the French Palace of Versailles, Peter the Great set about creating this grand imperial complex of palaces and gardens in the early 18th century. It was later expanded by his daughter, Tsarina Elizabeth.

Peterhof, the "Russian Versailles"

5 Smolnyy Convent
MAP G2 ■ Ploshchad Rastrelli 3/1 ■ Smolny Cathedral: 900 7015; open 7am–8pm daily

Tsarina Elizabeth founded this convent in 1748 and planned to see out her days here, but died before its completion. Upon the ascension of Catherine the Great, the convent became Russia's first girls' school. A stunning 19th-century cathedral with a dome and cupolas topped by gold orbs is its crowning glory.

Baroque interior of Catherine Palace, Tsarskoe Selo

⑥ Tsarskoe Selo

Developed into an imperial country residence by Peter the Great's wife, Catherine I, Tsarskoe Selo (see pp32–3) comprises vast areas of parkland and two stunning palaces. The striking Baroque Catherine Palace, designed by Bartolomeo Rastrelli, is the centrepiece of the estate. It is best known for its replica of the opulent Amber Room, which was looted by Nazis during World War II. The Neo-Classical Alexander Palace is currently closed for restoration.

Façade of Pavlovsk

⑦ Pavlovsk

Presented to Pavel I by his mother Catherine the Great in 1777, this royal estate contains over 1,000 acres of parkland and a fine palace designed by Scottish architect Charles Cameron. Though less extravagant than the palaces at nearby Tsarskoe Selo, Pavlovsk (see pp34–5) is well worth visiting to view the palace interior and the delightful English-style landscaped gardens.

⑧ Alexander Nevskiy Monastery

MAP G5 ▪ Ploshchad Aleksandra Nevskovo ▪ 274 1702 ▪ Open 9:30am–6pm daily

This sprawling monastery complex was founded in 1710 by Peter the Great on the supposed site of the 1240 battle between Russia and Sweden. It contains the early 18th-century Cathedral of the Annunciation, as well as the twin-towered and domed Neo-Classical Holy Trinity Cathedral, which houses the remains of Nevskiy, a revered 16th-century saint of Russia. The monastery is also home to two cemeteries, Lazarus and

---

THE AMBER ROOM

Completed in 1770, the magnificent Amber Room in Tsarskoe Selo was created by designer Rastrelli using amber mosaic panels gifted by the King of Prussia, surrounded by gilded carving, mirrors and gemstones. The Nazis took the contents of the room in 1941; the originals were never recovered. Work began in 1982 to re-create the Amber Room, and it was reopened in 2003.

Tikhvin, the latter containing the graves of Dostoevsky (see p46) and the 19th-century composer Pyotr Tchaikovsky.

⑨ Monument to the Heroic Defenders of Leningrad
MAP H1 ■ Ploshchad Pobedi

The World War II siege (see p38) had a colossal effect upon the mentality of the *blokadniki* (survivors) and upon the nature of the city itself. This monument, dedicated to the victims of the *blokada* (blockade), both alive and dead, consists of massive, resolute figures carved from granite.

Monument to the Heroic Defenders of Leningrad

⑩ Chesma Church
MAP H1 ■ Ulitsa Lensoveta 12 ■ Open 10am–7pm

The Neo-Gothic Chesma Church, with its wedding-cake façade, is one of the city's most distinctive churches. Built between 1777 and 1780, it was named in honour of the Russian naval victory over Turkey at Chesma in 1770 and used as a museum dedicated to the battle during the Soviet era. Opposite is the Chesma Palace, built between 1774 and 1777.

Chesma Church

See map on p100 ←

THREE EXCURSIONS

▶ **TRIP 1**

At the vast **Piskarevskoe Memorial Cemetery** (see p101), start with a visit to the Siege of Leningrad exhibition hall. Then make your way down the avenue leading to the heroic Mother Russia statue. Those able to read Russian should examine the verses on the wall behind, composed by a survivor of the siege (see p38). The 186 grassy mounds located on either side of the avenue are mass graves containing the bodies of the siege victims. A red star indicates that the graves hold soldiers; a hammer and sickle, civilians.

▶ **TRIP 2**

Begin your visit at the **Monument to the Heroic Defenders of Leningrad** and spend some time taking in the symbolic 48-m (157-ft) high granite obelisk before wandering among the colossal sculptures depicting the suffering brought to the city by World War II. Then make your way through the dimly lit underpass to the Memorial Hall. Inside the hall, look out for the display that contains a tiny crust of bread – the daily ration during the siege.

▶ **TRIP 3**

Walk down the Neva embankment towards **Ploschad Lenina**, where the famous 1926 **Statue of Lenin** (see p42) stands. Next, walk across to **Finland Station** (see p101) to see the train that brought Lenin to Russia to lead the 1917 Revolution. At nearby Ploshchad Lenina Metro Station, view an intricate Soviet-era Lenin mosaic.

Restaurants

PRICE CATEGORIES
For a three-course meal for one with half a bottle of wine, taxes and extra charges.

₽ under ₽4,000 ₽₽ ₽4,000–8,000
₽₽₽ over ₽8,000

1 Vody Lagidze
MAP E3 ▪ Ulitsa Belinskovo 3
▪ 579 1104 ▪ ₽
Opened at the end of the 1970s, when restaurants were rare in the city, Lagidze serves tasty Georgian food.

2 O Cuba!
MAP P5 ▪ Rubinshteyna ulitsa 36 ▪ 312 8892 ▪ ₽
A small slice of the tropics, this place serves barbecued meats and fresh seafood accompanied by powerful rum drinks. You can also enjoy a real Cuban cigar here.

3 Ukrop
MAP E3 ▪ Ulitsa Vossataniya 47 ▪ 946 3039 ▪ ₽
This vegetarian and raw vegan restaurant with a quirky interior is a welcome alternative to Russia's typically meat-based cuisine.

4 Korovabar
Holiday Inn Moskovskiye Vorota, Moskovskiy Prospekt 97A
▪ 388 3025 ▪ ₽₽
This smart restaurant has a reputation for excellent steaks.

5 Porto Maltese
MAP G5 ▪ Nevskiy prospekt 174 ▪ 271 7677 ▪ ₽₽
Mediterranean cuisine in a nautical setting. Choose from the display of seafood, and the chef does the rest.

6 Finnegan's
Moskovskiy pr. 192 ▪ 337 5755 ▪ ₽
A popular Irish bar with a good choice of beers. The menu includes Irish beef stroganoff and Russian-influenced dumpling dishes.

7 Pelmenia
MAP E4 ▪ Marata ulitsa 8 ▪ 415 4102 ▪ ₽
Named after Russian *pelmeni* (see p56), Pelmenia specializes in dumplings of various nations including Italian, Georgian and Chinese.

8 Buddha Bar
MAP G3 ▪ Sinopskaya naberezhnaya 78 ▪ 318 0707 ▪ ₽₽
The place to be seen in the city. Enjoy inventive cocktails along with contemporary Asian fusion cuisine.

9 Botanica
MAP P2 ▪ Ulitsa Pestelya 7 ▪ 272 7091 ▪ ₽
Vegetarians are well catered for at Botanica, which is welcoming of kids and turns out fresh, inventive dishes.

10 Nevskaya Zhemchuzhina
MAP G5 ▪ Obukhovskoy Oborony prospekt 26 ▪ 412 3120 ▪ ₽
Perched on the bank of the Neva, Russian fare is delivered to indoor and outdoor tables that have fantastic views of the river.

Bright seating area at Ukrop

Clubs and Bars

 Bar 812
MAP F4 ▪ Ulitsa Zhukovskovo 11 ▪ 956 8129

Bar 812 continues to impress with traditional cocktails and a range of "eko-cocktails" made from vegetables and fresh fruit.

 Tartarbar
MAP E3 ▪ Vilensky Pereulok 15 ▪ 7 911 922 5606 ▪ ₽

A gastronomic paradise, Tartarbar offers highly praised tartars and a variety of wines. It is better to book in advance.

3 Loft Project Etagi
MAP E5 ▪ Ligovskiy prospekt 74 ▪ 458 5005 ▪ Adm

This multifunctional art space occupies five floors of an old industrial bakery. It features exhibition areas, a slow-food café, a rooftop viewing point and Sever Bar, which serves teas and cocktails.

4 Zal
MAP B6 ▪ Nab. Obvodnogo Kanala 118 ▪ 407 3770 ▪ Adm

In the basement of an elegant 19th-century railway station, this popular club attracts international and local musicians on the more experimental end of the spectrum.

5 Griboedov
MAP E6 ▪ Voronezhskaya 2A ▪ 764 4355 ▪ Adm

Located in a former bomb shelter, this arty venue hosts live music and experimental DJs.

6 Kosmonavt
MAP D6 ▪ Bronnitskaya ulitsa 24 ▪ 929 3339 ▪ Box office open noon–9pm ▪ Adm

Housed in a former cinema, this club has live music by cutting-edge Russian and international artists.

The Jazz Philharmonic Harmonic Hall

7 St Petersburg State Jazz Philharmonic Hall
MAP P5 ▪ Zagorodnyy prospekt 27 ▪ 764 8565 ▪ Concerts start at 7pm

This sophisticated venue hosts concerts by established members of St Petersburg's thriving jazz scene.

8 Blok
MAP F3 ▪ Potyomkinskaya ulitsa 4 ▪ 389 5344 ▪ ₽₽

Set on the roof of the Leningrad Center in Tavrichesky Garden, Blok is known for its Russian meat dishes.

9 JFC Jazz Club
MAP E2 ▪ Shpalernaya ulitsa 33 ▪ 272 9850 ▪ Adm

An intimate, smoke-filled club dedicated to different styles of jazz. Arrive early to secure one of the coveted tables.

10 Foggy Dew
MAP E3 ▪ Ulitsa Vosstaniya 39 ▪ 273 6263

This authentic-looking Irish bar serves good, if slightly expensive, lunches. It has very friendly bar staff and offers good service. Locals and expats as well as tourists flock here at weekends.

See map on p100 ←

Streetsmart

Long escalators at Pushkinskaya station

Getting To and Around St Petersburg

Arriving by Air

Located 23 km south of the city, **Pulkovo Airport**'s Terminal 1, opened in 2014, is a splendid new facility that serves as St Petersburg's domestic and international airport. Buses and minibuses (marshrutka) depart every 10 to 15 minutes from outside the arrivals hall to Moskovsyaka metro station (20 minutes), from where it's a 20-minute journey into the city centre. Avoid using the unofficial taxis that lurk near the arrivals hall – licensed Pulkovo Taxis can be pre-booked from counters within the airport; the fare is around 1,000 roubles.

Airport facilities include free Wi-Fi, baby-changing rooms, and lifts and toilets for passengers with disabilities. There are also cafés, duty-free shops, ATMs and bureaux de change. **Turkish Airlines** and **Air Baltic**, the Latvian budget carrier, currently offer the cheapest flights between St Petersburg and a number of European capitals.

Arriving by Boat

The journey by boat from Moscow takes around two weeks and can be arranged through **Go Russia**.

Regular ferries running between St Petersburg and Helsinki (10 hours), Tallinn (14 hours) and Stockholm (24 hours) can be booked via **St Peter**

Line. Large cruise ships dock at Marine Facade Port on the western tip of Vasilevskiy Island, while smaller ships dock at either Naberezhnaya Leytenenta Shmidta on the eastern side of Vasilevskiy Island or opposite at the English Embankment.

Arriving by Train

There are many trains from Moscow to Moscow station (Moskovskiy vokzal) in St Petersburg, including an express train (Sapsan) that takes just under 4 hours. However, the most popular trains are the sleepers, which take over 8 hours. You can travel by platzkarte, coupe or SV, which are, respectively, a seat in a carriage, a berth in a four-person cabin, and a bed in a two-person cabin.

Timetables can be found on the **Russian Railways** website. Several daily express trains link Helsinki with Finland Station (Finlyandskiy vokzal) in St Petersburg (3 hours and 30 minutes); tickets can be booked on the **VR** website.

Travelling by Metro

The city's metro is incredibly good value and trains come at regular intervals, ranging from every 3 minutes during rush hour, to every 4 or 5 minutes late at night. The metro is open until midnight, although trains continue

to run until 12:30am. More than just a mode of public transport, St Petersburg's metro is an attraction in its own right (see pp48–9).

Travelling by Bus

Bus stops are identifiable by their white-and-yellow signs with a red "A" (for avtobus). These buses can be very crowded during rush hour. Slightly more expensive, privately run buses add a "K" before their bus numbers, which are the same as those of the state-operated buses.

Travelling by Trolley Bus

Trolley buses, unlike trams, run up and down Nevskiy prospekt and, in this part of the city at least, are a convenient and cheap mode of transport. But they can get crowded and, like trams, often break down. Blue-and-white signs mark the stops.

Travelling by Minibus

Minibuses (marshrutka) are privately run and travel around the city, following standard bus routes; they can be hailed by waving your hand. Pay the driver when you get in or take your seat and pass the money on.

Travelling by Tram

Trams (tramvai) are popular all over the

former Soviet Union, and St Petersburg is no exception. The stops are identifiable by the red-and-white signs above the tram rails. Less crowded than buses, they are a great way to see the city. However, they tend to break down frequently.

Tickets and Travel Cards

All modes of transport run on a flat-fare system. Regular tickets can be bought from conductors or drivers on buses, trolley buses and trams. To use the metro, buy a token (zheton) from the ticket offices (kassa) within each station. If you plan to make several trips, a more convenient and cheaper option is to buy the electronic traffic card called the Podorozhnik card. This rechargeable card can be bought at metro ticket offices. You can add a certain amount of money to it and use it by placing it on the electronic readers. It works for every kind of public transport including metro, buses, trolley-buses and trams. Some cards are also valid for a couple of days.

Travelling by Car

Driving is not advised in St Petersburg, but if you do choose to travel by car, note that **Hertz**, **Avis**, **Sixt** and **Europcar** all offer car hire from Pulkovo Airport. In Russia, traffic drives on the right. Vehicles should not make any left turns on main roads unless a road sign indicates that this is permitted.

In winter, driving requires studded tyres as chains can be damaged on tram lines.

Tourists are required by law to have a notarized translation of their driving licence; producing an international driving licence will not suffice.

Travelling by Taxi

It's safest to avoid unofficial taxis and stick with reputable licensed taxi companies such as **Taksovichkoff**, **Taxi Vezyot**, **Uber** and **Yandex Taxi** that quote fixed prices and can be booked by phone. If the company you call doesn't have an English-speaking operator, staff in a restaurant, bar or hotel will be happy to make a booking for you.

Travelling by Bicycle

St Petersburg is flat and compact and should be a haven for cyclists; however, the city also attracts a lot of reckless drivers. If you choose to cycle, wear a helmet and stick to quieter streets.

Bikes can be rented from **Skat Prokat** and **Velotour**, who also lead cycling tours.

Travelling on Foot

St Petersburg is an excellent city for walking. Many of the main sights, especially those at the city's centre, are close together, making it easy to travel from one to the other by foot.

Street signs are in both Russian and English in the centre, Russian only in the outskirts. Many of

the English signs were erected in time for the city's 300th anniversary celebrations in 2003.

DIRECTORY

ARRIVING BY AIR

Air Baltic
w airbaltic.com

Pulkovo Airport
w pulkovoairport.ru

Turkish Airlines
w turkishairlines.com

ARRIVING BY BOAT

Go Russia
w justgorussia.co.uk

St Peter Line
w stpeterline.com

ARRIVING BY TRAIN

Russian Railways
w rzd.ru

VR
w vr.fi

TRAVELLING BY CAR

Avis
w avis.com

Europcar
w europcar.com

Hertz
w hertz.com

Sixt
w sixt.com

TRAVELLING BY TAXI

Taxi Vezyot
c 318 0318
w spb.rutaxi.ru

Taxovichkof
c 333 0000
w taxovichkof.ru

Uber
w uber.com/ru/

Yandex Taxi
c 366 6666
w taxi.yandex.ru

TRAVELLING BY BICYCLE

Skat Prokat
Goncharnaya ulitsa 7
c 717 6838
w skatprokat.ru

Velotour
c 981 0155
w velotour-spb.ru

Practical Information

Passports and Visas

All visitors from the US, Canada, the EU, Australia and New Zealand need to obtain a visa from Russian Visa Centres in their home country before travelling to Russia. Passports must be valid for a minimum of 6 months after the visa expiry date.

While British and Danish citizens have to submit their visa applications in person and provide biometric data, citizens of most other countries can have their visa applications submitted by an agent or by mail. Independent travellers must provide proof of their hotel reservation and those visitors staying at private homes need to produce an official invitation from their host.

Cruise-ship passengers and passengers on ferries from Helsinki and Tallinn are entitled to stay in St Petersburg for up to 72 hours without a visa. Those on cruise ships must sleep on board and can only visit the city in the company of an official guide; passengers arriving by ferry must book accommodation in the city.

Customs and Immigration

All visitors are given an immigration card upon arrival. This has to be kept for the entire duration of the visit and shown to the police on request. Photocopies are not usually accepted. You are also required to carry your passport at all times.

By law you have to register with the Federal Migration Service within 7 days of your arrival in Russia. Hotels will handle this for their guests; those staying in private homes must be registered by their host. Registration receipts should be kept with your passport and immigration card. If you are carrying cash or antiques, valuable jewellery, laptops, or other electrical equipment over the value of US$3,000 upon entry to Russia, you will need to fill out a customs declaration form. You will need to present it when you leave, so that you can take the items back with you.

It is against the law to export objects over 50 years old from Russia, so try to avoid buying anything that looks remotely antique during your stay.

Travel Safety Advice

Visitors can get up-to-date safety information from the **UK Foreign and Commonwealth Office**, the **US Department of State** and the **Australian Department of Foreign Affairs and Trade**.

Travel Insurance

Although it's not obligatory to have a travel insurance policy for a trip to Russia, it is advisable to take out an insurance policy that covers cancellation or curtailment of your trip, theft or loss of baggage, and healthcare.

Health insurance is particularly important as the country's public hospitals are generally not up to Western standards. Private health care is excellent, but it can be very expensive.

Health

If you become ill, speak to someone at your hotel reception or contact the **CLINIC MEDSI** or the **American Medical Clinic and Hospital**, which both specialize in dealing with foreigners and operate 24 hours.

Pharmacies *(apteka)* are very easy to find, and many of them are open 24 hours. However, it is a good idea to bring essential medicines and prescriptions with you, as they may be sold under different names at the local pharmacies.

For dental issues, the MEDEM clinic provides most dentistry services, but they are not cheap. An alternative is to ask your hotel to find you an English-speaking dentist.

Visitors are advised to drink bottled water. The tap water in St Petersburg contains heavy metals and *giardia*, a parasite causing stomach problems.

Personal Security

As in any large city, take all the precautions that you normally would to protect yourself. Avoid walking alone at night and keep your valuables in a safe place. Watch out for scams, but try not to be too paranoid.

Petty crime can be a problem in St Petersburg, and pickpockets are known to operate on buses and the metro. Be on your guard and keep your belongings close. If you do have property stolen, you will need to report it to the local police station for insurance purposes. Take all your documents with you (passport, visa and migration card). You may also be asked to write a statement. If this is the case, ask your hotel for assistance or call the Tourist Helpline; they should be able to help provide an interpreter.

Emergency Services

For emergencies, the **police**, **ambulance** service and **fire brigade** each have a dedicated phone number, but the operators may not speak English.

The English-language **Tourist Helpline** should also be able to provide assistance. You may wish to consider contacting your consulate (if there is one in St Petersburg) or your embassy in Moscow if you have a particularly serious problem.

Travellers with Specific Needs

The city is severely lacking in facilities for the disabled, although the situation is improving. Of the museums, only the Hermitage and the Russian Museum have disabled access. Several four- and five-star hotels are now equipped for disabled guests, but you should call ahead to check the situation before you book your accommodation.

Liberty provides tours around St Petersburg and its suburbs for disabled travellers. They use minibuses with lifts and

folding ramps to transport wheelchair users around the city, and can also advise on the best restaurants with disabled facilities.

Currency

Russia's currency is the rouble (₽), written рубль. One rouble is divided into 100 kopeks (100k). There are eight denominations of notes, with values of ₽10, ₽50, ₽100, ₽200, ₽500, ₽1,000, ₽2,000 and ₽5,000. There are also eight coins: ₽10, ₽5, ₽2, ₽1, 50k, 10k, 5k and 1k.

Time Difference

St Petersburg follows Moscow Time, which is 4 hours ahead of Greenwich Mean Time (GMT), and 9 hours ahead of Eastern Standard Time (EST). Russia does not observe Daylight Saving Time.

DIRECTORY

PASSPORTS AND VISAS

Australian Consulate
MAP A2 ■ 14 Petrovskiy prospekt █ 325 7334
ⓦ sydneyrussian consulate.com/en/visa-section.html

Canada
ⓦ canada-ils.com

UK
ⓦ ru.vfsglobal.co.uk

US
ⓦ ils-usa.com

TRAVEL SAFETY ADVICE

Australian Department of Foreign Affairs and Trade
ⓦ dfat.gov.au
ⓦ smarttraveller.gov.au

UK Foreign and Commonwealth Office
ⓦ gov.uk/foreign-travel-advice

US Department of State
ⓦ travel.state.gov

HEALTH

American Medical Clinic and Hospital
MAP J4 ■ Nab. Reki Moyki 78
█ 740 2090
ⓦ www.amclinic.com

CLINIC MEDSI
MAP C1 ■ Ulitsa Marata 6
█ 643 5273
ⓦ medem.ru

EMERGENCY

Ambulance
03

Fire Brigade
01

Police
112

Tourist Helpline
█ 303 0555

TRAVELLERS WITH SPECIFIC NEEDS

Liberty
MAP B1 ■ Ulitsa Polozova 12
█ 232 8163
ⓦ libertytour.ru

Opening Hours

Most sights are open from 10:30am until 6pm, with no break for lunch. Shops are open from 10am until 8 to 10pm, 7 days a week, and there are a number of 24-hour shops, ranging from simple grocery stores to hip boutiques. Parks are usually open from 10am until 10pm, with opening hours extended during White Nights.

Visitor Information

Visit Petersburg is the official tourist organization for St Petersburg. There are information kiosks throughout the city, but the main tourism offices are in Sadovaya ulitsa and Sennaya Square. For a full list of visitor centres, plus information on sights, events and accommodation, go to the Visit Petersburg website.

Other useful sources of information include **Saint-Petersburg.com** and **St Petersburg in Your Pocket**.

Trips and Tours

One of the best ways to see St Petersburg is to tour its many canals and rivers. English-language tours are offered by companies such as **Astra Marine**, **Neptun-boat** and **Anglotourismo**.

Buying a day ticket to use the hop-on hop-off **City Tour** buses is one of the most convenient land-based sightseeing options as it's a flexible way to take in the main sights of your choice.

The **St Petersburg Free Tour** is an enjoyable 2-hour walking tour with a professional guide. These can be very useful and informative, but note that the guide will be appreciative of a generous tip.

Cyclists can join a 3-hour guided city bike tour run by **Skatprokat**, which also rents out bikes by the hour or day.

Numerous other local travel agents such as **Anastasia Travel Group** and **Maxi Balt Tours** organize a variety of guided city tours that include mini-bus trips and even helicopter flights.

Shopping

Although still not quite on a par with Moscow, St Petersburg's shopping scene has plenty to offer. Nevskiy prospekt remains the city's commercial heart with its profusion of shopping arcades and souvenir, food and clothing shops, along with the grand **Gostinyy Dvor** shopping mall, home to the city's most expensive boutiques.

With its historic façade and hundreds of shops, the **Galeria** shopping mall is a great central option.

The ubiquitous Russian nesting dolls (*matryoshki*) are an obvious souvenir choice, as is amber jewellery from the Baltic region. Decorative lacquer boxes and imperial china designs produced by the **Imperial Porcelain Factory** are also popular, and Russian chocolates in pretty wrappers make great gifts for children.

Avoid buying art, antiques, musical instruments, fur or expensive items of jewellery in St Petersburg as these are usually subject to strict export controls (*see p110*). You can secure permission to export unique books and art objects from the **Ministry of Culture**, and the process for this is relatively speedy.

VAT is included in the price of all items you buy in Russia, but it cannot be claimed back at the border as in some European countries.

If you need to ship large items home, **DHL** is probably the best option as they can also arrange customs clearances if necessary.

Dining

The city has a broad choice of cuisine, from restaurants once serving dishes once enjoyed by the Russian aristocracy to food from the former Soviet republics of Georgia, Armenia and Azerbaijan.

Zakuski (appetisers), are usually eaten cold before the main meal. These could be salads, marinated mushrooms, pancakes, pickled herring or gherkins. They are usually served with bread and sour cream. There are also specific *zakuski* to accompany beer and vodka, including dried, salted fish, dried squid and anchovies.

The city's main restaurant areas are Nevskiy prospekt and

the surrounding streets, and the area around the Mariinskiy Theatre.

Most restaurants and cafés open around noon. Many stay open until the last guest leaves, but some close their doors from around 11pm. In several top-end hotels, restaurants open for breakfast, as do many cafés in the city. Alcohol can be bought 24 hours a day.

English-language menus can be found in the majority of restaurants in the centre, but further afield they are likely to be in Russian only.

It is common practice to tip the waiting staff in restaurants – 10 to 15 per cent of the bill will suffice.

Vegetarians used to have a very hard time in St Petersburg, but the city now has a good choice of vegetarian and vegan restaurants as well as cafés.

In more upmarket restaurants, it is usually advisable to book ahead, especially during the White Nights Festival (see p62), when tables can be booked up weeks or even months in advance.

Accommodation

St Petersburg has accommodation to suit all tastes and budgets, from sociable hostels with dorm rooms to lavish historic hotels in palatial buildings.

The main five-star hotels are located in the centre, on and around Nevskiy prospekt, but there are some good hotels further out as well. Expect impeccably clean rooms, efficient service, en-suite air-conditioned rooms as well as free Wi-Fi from both international chains and privately-run hotels recommended in this guide.

Short-stay apartments with kitchen facilities are a good alternative option for families or small groups and can often be found in central locations.

Note that some of the top establishments in the city have metal detectors and bag searches at their entrances. This is simply a precaution for the protection of guests, and is not something to be overly concerned about.

Most hotels have an online booking system and should be able to assist guests with visa support prior to their arrival in Russia.

International hotel reservation sites, such as **Booking.com**, and **Hotels.com** can be a useful tool for finding the best places to stay in the city, but it is worth checking the hotel's own website before you book, as this can often offer the best deals or promotions.

Payments can be made in the top hotels by credit card or cash. In smaller hotels, cash may be your only option. Be aware that some hotels do not include local taxes in the prices they quote. These can be a significant addition to the bill.

Prices increase significantly during the peak of the White Nights period – book well in advance for a trip during this time.

DIRECTORY

VISITOR INFORMATION

Saint-Petersburg.com
Ⓦ saint-petersburg.com

St Petersburg in Your Pocket
Ⓦ inyourpocket.com/st-petersburg

Visit St Petersburg
Ⓦ visit-petersburg.ru/en

TRIPS AND TOURS

Anastasia Travel Group
Ⓦ anastasia.travel

Anglotourismo
Ⓦ anglotourismo.com

Astra Marine
Ⓦ astra-marine.ru

City Tour
Ⓦ citytourspb.ru

Maxi Balt Tours
Ⓦ maxibalttours.com

Neptun-boat
Ⓦ neptun-boat.ru

Skatprokat
Ⓦ skatprokat.ru

St Petersburg Free Tour
Ⓦ petersburgfreetour.com

SHOPPING

DHL
Ⓦ dhl.ru

Galeria
MAP E5 ▪ Ligovskiy prospekt 30A

Gostinyy Dvor
MAP N4 ▪ Nevskiy prospekt 35

Imperial Porcelain Factory
Ⓦ ipm.ru

Ministry of Culture
MAP K3 ▪ Ministerstvo Kultury, Malaya Morskaya ulitsa 17
Ⓦ mkrf.ru

ACCOMMODATION

Booking.com
Ⓦ booking.com

Hotels.com
Ⓦ hotels.com

Places to Stay

PRICE CATEGORIES
For a standard double room per night in high season
(with breakfast if included), taxes and extra charges.

₽ under ₽10,000 ₽₽ ₽10,000–₽20,000 ₽₽₽ over ₽20,000

Luxury Hotels

Corinthia Hotel
St Petersburg
MAP E4 ▪ Nevskiy
prospekt 57 ▪ 380 2001
▪ www. corinthia.com ▪ ₽₽
Ideally located, this hotel
has a range of superb
restaurants and shops.
The Imperial restaurant's
Sunday brunch is also
open to non-guests.

Radisson Royal Hotel
MAP E4 ▪ Nevskiy
prospekt 49/2 ▪ 322 5000
▪ www.radisson.ru ▪ ₽₽
Part of the well-known
international chain, this
hotel is close to major
sights. It also houses
a fitness centre with
top-quality service. The
floor-to-ceiling windows
of the cafés and rooms
offer great views of
Nevskiy prospekt.

Renaissance
St Petersburg Baltic
MAP J4 ▪ Pochtamtskaya
ulitsa 4 ▪ 380 4000 ▪ www.
marriott.com ▪ ₽₽
An atmospheric hotel
in one of the city's oldest
areas, the Renaissance is
a luxury hotel with char-
acter. Part of the Marriott
chain, it contains a fitness
club and a restaurant.

Astoria
MAP K4 ▪ Bolshaya
Morskaya ulitsa 39 ▪ 494
5757 ▪ www.roccoforte
hotels.com ▪ ₽₽₽
Set in an area of the city
that is quiet yet central,

Astoria's front rooms
offer great views of
St Isaac's Square.

Belmond Grand
Hotel Europe
MAP N3 ▪ Mikhaylovskaya
ulitsa 1/7 ▪ 329 6000
▪ www.belmond.com/ru/
grand-hotel-europe-st-
petersburg/ ▪ ₽₽₽
The Grand Hotel Europe's
historic opulent interiors,
as well as its fine restaurants and bars, make it one
of the top places to stay in
the city. Established more
than a century ago, the
hotel is an institution.

Four Seasons Hotel
Lion Palace
MAP K3 ▪ Voznesenskiy
prospekt 1 ▪ 399 8000
▪ www.fourseasons.com/
stpetersburg ▪ ₽₽₽
Formerly a palace, this
luxury hotel is directly
opposite St Isaac's
Cathedral. All rooms
have spectacular views.
The rooftop pool and
terrace bar are perfect
for watching sunsets.

Kempinski Hotel
Moika
MAP M2 ▪ Nab. reki
Moyki 22 ▪ 335 9111
▪ www.kempinksi.com
▪ ₽₽₽
One of the city's most
popular upmarket hotels,
the Kempinski is just
a few steps from the
Hermitage. It is part of a
German chain and has
a splendid restaurant
with great views.

SO Sofitel
St Petersburg
MAP K3 ▪ Voznesenskiy
prospekt 6 ▪ 610 6161
▪ www.sofitel.com/gb/
hotel-B315-so-sofitel-st-
petersburg-/index.shtml
▪ ₽₽₽
Formerly known as the W,
this hotel is located at the
city's cultural centre. Take
in spectacular views of
the St Isaac's cathedral
from the terrace, and enjoy
the SO evening parties.

Taleon Imperial
MAP M2 ▪ Nab. Reki
Moyki 59 ▪ 324 9911
▪ www.taleon.ru ▪ ₽₽₽
Occupying a former
palace, this is one of the
few hotels that arranges
events for children. Every
guest is given their own
personal valet with rooms
overlooking the Moyka river.

Historic Hotels

3 MostA
MAP N2 ▪ Nab. Reki
Moyki 3 ▪ 611 1188
▪ www.3mosta.com ▪ ₽
A delightful hotel just a
few minutes' walk from
the Hermitage. Breakfasts
are generous, with splen-
did views of the Church
on Spilled Blood from
the breakfast room.

Art Hotel
Rachmaninov
MAP M4 ▪ Kazanskaya
ulitsa 5 ▪ 571
9778 ▪ www.hotel
rachmaninov.com ▪ ₽
Housed in the former
residence of the Russian
composer Rachmaninov,
this hotel is furnished with
antiques. Located close
to the major sights, it is
surprisingly good value.

Brothers Karamazov

MAP D5
■ Sotsialisticheskaya ulitsa 11a ■ 335 1185 ■ www.karamazovhotel.ru ■ ₽
A must for Dostoevsky enthusiasts, Brothers Karamazov is located close to the museum dedicated to the writer's life (see p46). Each room is named after a female character in one of his works.

Oktiabrskaya

MAP E4 ■ Ligovskiy prospekt 10 ■ 578 1515 ■ www.oktober-hotel.spb.ru ■ ₽
This huge central hotel was first opened in 1851, when it was famed for its state-of-the-art technology. It now has bright spacious rooms with classical style furniture.

Pushkinsky Domik

MAP A6 ■ Nab. Kanala Griboedova 174a ■ 710 8351 ■ www.pushkin-hotel.com ■ ₽
This inexpensive hotel prides itself on the fact that Pushkin (see p46) wrote many of his famous works during his stay here in 1816–18. The hotel is a genuine architectural treasure, unaltered since the 19th century.

Angleterre

MAP K4 ■ Malaya Morskaya 24 ■ 494 5666 ■ www.angleterrehotel.com ■ ₽₽
This upmarket hotel is famous for being the planned venue for the Nazi's "Victory Ball" after the fall of St Petersburg during WWII – fortunately, the city never capitulated. The rooms here are exceptionally comfortable.

Rossi Boutique Hotel

MAP D5 ■ Nab. Reki Fontanki 55 ■ 635 6333 ■ www.rossihotels.com ■ ₽₽
In the heart of Sennaya ploshchad, this highly rated hotel is housed in a 19th-century bulding. Its elegant rooms feature exposed ceiling beams, wood panelling and tiled floors. The service is excellent.

Solo Sokos Hotel Palace Bridge

MAP B3 ■ Birzhevoi pereulok 2-4 ■ 335 2200 ■ www.sokoshotels.fi/ru ■ ₽₽
Belonging to the Finnish chain of Sokos Hotels, this hotel is located at the city centre on Vasilyevsky Island. It houses a spa, a fitness centre as well as the restaurant Dans le Noir.

The State Hermitage Museum Official Hotel

MAP A3 ■ Ulitsa Pravdy 10 ■ 777 9810 ■ www.thehermitagehotel.ru ■ ₽₽₽
Not within the Hermitage, but palatial nonetheless, this hotel gives guests a flavour of old Russian royal family life. It boasts large luxuriously furnished rooms as well as flawless service.

Business Hotels

Alexander House

MAP J6 ■ Nab. Kryukova Kanala 27 ■ 575 3877 ■ www.a-house.ru ■ ₽
This hotel takes pride in its spacious and elegant rooms – two luxury suites even boast working fireplaces. Reconstructed in the style of a 19th-century gentleman's house, the hotel also has a small bar and restaurant.

Crowne Plaza St. Petersburg Ligovsky

MAP E5 ■ Ligovsky prospekt 61 ■ 8 800 500 9842 ■ www.ihg.com ■ ₽
Located conveniently close to Moskovskiy railway station and Nevskiy prospekt, this hotel offers clean and quiet rooms, extensive business facilities and good breakfasts.

Park Inn by Radisson Pribaltiyskaya Hotel & Congress Center

Korablestroiteley ulitsa 14 ■ 329 2626 ■ www.parkinn.ru ■ ₽
This Soviet colossus is away from the city centre. However, it offers good business facilities and is perfect for walks along the Gulf of Finland. Be sure to ask for a room with a view of the gulf.

Park Inn by Radisson Pulkovskaya Hotel

MAP G2 ■ Pobedy ploshchad 1 ■ 740 3900 ■ www.parkinn.com/hotelpulkovskaya-stpetersburg ■ ₽
Not far from the airport, this hotel makes a good base for exploring the city, and is convenient for day trips to Pavlovsk and Tsarskoe Selo. It has its own bakery and brewery.

Casa Leto

MAP C4 ■ Bolshaya Morskaya ulitsa 34 ■ 600 1096 ■ www.casaleto.com ■ ₽₽
Located in a historic building with stripped wooden floors and period features, this family-run hotel is close to the city's top sights and has large pleasant rooms. Its accommodating staff make for an enjoyable stay.

Helvetia Hotel & Suites

MAP E5 ▪ Ulitsa Marata 11 ▪ 326 5353 ▪ www.helvetia hotel.ru ▪ ₽₽

Set in a quiet courtyard, this hotel is further away from the city centre, but it is within walking distance of the major sights. The family rooms have their own kitchen equipment.

Petro Palace

MAP L3 ▪ Malaya Morskaya ulitsa 14 ▪ 571 3006 ▪ www.petropalace hotel.com ▪ ₽₽

Housed in a 19th-century building, this hotel is popular with wealthier Russians and European business travellers. It has a fitness centre and pool.

Mid-Range Hotels

Azimut Hotel

MAP B5 ▪ Lermontovskiy prospekt 43/1 ▪ 200 0048 ▪ www.azimuthotels.com ▪ ₽

The glitzy Azimut is unexpectedly inexpensive, and is a taxi ride or a tram journey away from major sights. The hotel offers a wide range of rooms.

Kvartira N4 Ginza Project

MAP B2 ▪ Syezzhinskaya ulitsa 38 ▪ 640 1616 ▪ www.kvartira-n-4-ginza-project.allpiterhotels.ru ▪ ₽

This characterful hotel features retro decor. The 1970s-style wallpaper and furniture design is combined with modern facilities and high service standards.

Matisov Domik

MAP A5 ▪ Nab. Reki Pryazhki 3/1 ▪ 495 0242 ▪ www.matisov.com ▪ ₽

Popular with many famous Russian actors, this cosy three-star hotel is not well served by public transport but guests can take a taxi or a long walk to the centre of town. The hotel also provides a free shuttle bus on weekdays.

Okhtinskaya

MAP G2 ▪ Bolsheokhtinskiy prospekt 4 ▪ 318 0040 ▪ www.okhtinskaya.com ▪ ₽

This hotel is a little out of the way, but it runs shuttle buses to Nevskiy prospekt. There is a danger of being partly cut off in summer when the drawbridges are raised, so guests should be aware of the timings for this. The building is modern and the rooms are spacious.

Stony Island Hotel

MAP C1 ▪ Kamennoostrovskiy prospekt 45 ▪ 337 2434 ▪ www.stonyisland.ru ▪ ₽

A good-value, modern hotel a little way out from the centre, Stony Island has a good restaurant-bar and buffet breakfast.

Tuchkov Hotel

MAP A2 ▪ Malyy prospekt Vasilevskogo Ostrova 7 ▪ 240 2731 ▪ www.tuchkov-hotel.ru ▪ ₽

Close to a metro station, this mini-hotel is highly rated for its cleanliness, comfort and service. The free pastries are a welcome perk.

Ekaterina Art Hotel

MAP M2 ▪ Millionnaya ulitsa 10A ▪ 401 6566 ▪ www.ekaterinahotel. com ▪ ₽₽

This atmospheric hotel has an enviable central location just minutes from the main sights. Occupying a historic building with plenty of period features, it also has an excellent restaurant on the ground floor.

Tavricheskaya Hotel

MAP G2 ▪ Shpalernaya ulitsa 53 ▪ 326 6772 ▪ www.tavrhotel.ru ▪ ₽₽

With basic features, this hotel is not for those seeking luxury. However, its location makes it a great base for sightseeing, especially for those on a budget. The rooms are clean and functional, and the staff are friendly.

Central Hotels

Arbat Nord

MAP E3 ▪ Artilleryskaya ulitsa 4 ▪ 200 8913 ▪ www.arbat-nord.ru ▪ ₽

The Arbat Nord attracts tourists, thanks to its prime location close to the Field of Mars *(see p75)*. Rooms are stylish and equipped with all amenities.

Arka Hotel

MAP M3 ▪ Bolshaya Konyushennaya 17/3 ▪ 272 6493 ▪ www. baskof-hotel.com ▪ ₽

Right in the heart of the historic centre, this great budget option has clean, simply furnished double and triple rooms with en-suite bathrooms. It's a very popular choice, so be sure to book well ahead.

Comfort Hotel

MAP K4 ▪ Bolshaya Morskaya ulitsa 25 ▪ 570 6700 ▪ www.comfort-hotel.org ▪ ₽

A real find, Comfort Hotel is reasonably priced and is set in an unbeatably central location, with simple yet spacious rooms.

Herzen House Hotel

MAP K4 ▪ Bolshaya Morskaya ulitsa 25 ▪ 315 5550 ▪ www.herzen-hotel.ru ▪ ₽

Located centrally, the Herzen offers clean, modestly furnished rooms at good value. Some rooms have lovely city views.

Hotel Shelfort

MAP A3 ▪ 3-ya liniya 26, Vasilevskiy Ostrov ▪ 328 0555 ▪ www.shelfort.ru ▪ ₽

Perfectly located for exploring the Strelka area of Vasilevskiy Island (see pp88–91), this no-frills hotel is within walking distance of the island's many sights.

Kronverk

MAP B2 ▪ Blokhina ulitsa 9 ▪ 703 3663 ▪ www.kronverk.com ▪ ₽

Superbly located for the Peter and Paul Fortress, Kronverk's rooms are pleasant and functional. Those who wish to stay longer can book one of the hotel's flats.

Nevskiy Hotel Grand

MAP M3 ▪ Bolshaya Konyushennaya ulitsa 10 ▪ 703 3860 ▪ www.hon.ru ▪ ₽

Set in the historic centre of the city, this three-star hotel offers a little bit of luxury at affordable rates. It has a range of comfortable rooms.

Puppet Theatre Hostel

MAP E3 ▪ Nekrasova ulitsa 14 ▪ 272 5401 ▪ www.hostel-puppet.ru ▪ ₽

Right in the centre of the city, just a short walk from Nevskiy prospekt, this inexpensive hotel has private rooms and dorms.

Petr Hotel

MAP C4 ▪ Admiralteyskiy prospekt 8 ▪ 315 2401 ▪ www.petr-hotel.com ▪ ₽₽

Since opening in 2014, this hotel has quickly gained a reputation for impeccable standards. Its large rooms are furnished in classic modern style, with most of them offering fine city views.

Pushka Inn

MAP M2 ▪ Nab. Reki Moyki 14 ▪ 644 7120 ▪ www.pushkainn.ru ▪ ₽₽

Close to the Hermitage, this inn is housed in an 18th-century building near the Moyka river. Set in the city's historical centre, the hotel is a fine medium-range choice, with friendly, English-speaking staff and a good on-site restaurant.

Budget Options

Azart Hotel

MAP F5 ▪ Nevskiy prospekt 136, apt 33 ▪ 002 8184 ▪ www.azart.allpiterhotels.ru/en ▪ ₽

Occupying a converted apartment in an old residential building, this small hotel has bright, cheerful rooms withen-suite bathrooms and use of a shared kitchen.

Cameo Hotel

MAP D5 ▪ Nab. Reki Fontanki 90 ▪ 328 1515 ▪ www.cameohotel.ru ▪ ₽

This quiet and simply decorated hotel is set within a courtyard garden. It has a cosy café and a 24-hour bar. The central riverside location makes it an ideal base from which to explore the city.

Hotel Anabel

MAP E4 ▪ Nevsky Prospekt 88 ▪ 400 2211 ▪ www.anabel.ru ▪ ₽

This cosy hotel is located close to the Moskovsky railway station. It is set in an old traditional yard that shields its rooms from the city noise.

Podushka Hostel

MAP E5 ▪ Marata ulitsa 33 ▪ 248 1716 ▪ www.podushka-hostel.com ▪ ₽

A lovely hostel with immaculate rooms and helpful staff. Guests have the use of a shared kitchen and can hire bicycles to explore the city.

Senat Inn

MAP E3 ▪ Kirochnaya ulitsa 12 ▪ 309 57600 ▪ www.senat-inn.allpiterhotels.ru ▪ ₽

Squeezed into a floor of a residential building, all the five rooms here have en-suite bathrooms and smart modern furniture. Chernyshevskaya metro station is nearby.

Simple Hostel

MAP C4 ▪ Gorokhovaya ulitsa 4 ▪ 385 2528 ▪ www.simplehostel.com ▪ ₽

In an excellent central location, this fantastic hostel has quirky interior design features that include entire bunk beds made from chipboard.

Sofia Hostel

MAP E5 ▪ Ulitsa Pushkinskaya 18 ▪ 251 3536 ▪ www.sofia-hostel.allpiterhotels.ru ▪ ₽

This delightful hostel has great facilities including a large self-catering kitchen and dining area. The comfortable, homely interior is kept spotless.

For a key to hotel price categories see p114

General Index

Acknowledgments

Author
Marc Bennetts was born in London, UK, and moved to St Petersburg in 1997, where he learned Russian. Marc also contributed to DK's *Eyewitness Travel Guide St Petersburg*. He now lives in Mosccow, not far from Red Square.

Additional Contributor
Matt Willis

Publishing Director Georgina Dee
Publisher Vivien Antwi
Design Director Phil Ormerod
Editorial Neha Chander, Michelle Crane, Rachel Fox, Rada Radojicic, Erin Richards, Sally Schafer, Sophie Wright
Cover Design Bess Daly, Maxine Pedliham
Design Tessa Bindloss, Richard Czapnik, Bharti Karakoti, Bhavika Mathur, Marisa Renzullo, Vinita Venugopal
Picture Research Susie Peachey, Ellen Root, Lucy Sienkowska, Oran Tarjan
Cartography Jasneet Kaur, Suresh Kumar, Casper Morris, Reetu Pandey
DTP Jason Little, George Nimmo
Production Nancy-Jane Maun
Factchecker Irina Titova
Proofreader Susanne Hillen
Indexer Helen Peters
First edition created by Quadrum Solutions, Mumbai
Revisions Sumita Khatwani, Shikha Kulkarni, Bandana Paul, Kanika Praharaj, Anuroop Sanwalia, Tanveer Zaidi
Commissioned Photography John Heseltine, Jon Spaull

Picture Credits
The publisher would like to thank the following for their kind permission to reproduce their photographs:

Key: a-above; b-below/bottom; c-centre; f-far; l-left; r-right; t-top

123RF.com: Nataliya Dvukhimenna 89bc; Marina Zezelina 96b.

Alamy Stock Photo: Art Directors & TRIP/ArkReligion.com/Vladimir Sidoropolev 95br; Bogomyako 50bc; Paul Brown 74b; Danita Delimont/Cindy Miller Hopkins 79br; Dainis Derics 28br; Peter Forsberg/Europe 103tl; Agata Gładykowska 56br; Bill Heinsohn 4b; hemis.fr/Camille Moirenc 19cr; Heritage Image Partnership Ltd/ Fine Art Images 67l; ITAR-TASS Photo Agency 12cla, 98cla;

ITAR-TASS News Agency 20bl, 98br, 105tr; John Kellerman 1b, 61br; Inga Leksina 94tl; Yadid Levy 95tl; Martin Lindsay 48b; Eric Nathan 3tr, 106-7; Alexander Perepelitsyn 80cl; Pictorial Press Ltd 47br; Natallia Rumiantseva 101tl; Maurice Savage 43br, 49c, 97tr; Michael Schultes 82b ; Alex Segre 73tr; Neil Setchfield102bl; Stock Connection Blue/Dallas and John Heaton 4cl; Geoffrey Taunton 48cl; TravelCollection/ Klaus Bossemeyer 71t; TravelCollection/Michael Holz 70bl; VPC Photo 91cl; Zoonar GmbH/Dmitriy Raykin 32-3.

AWL Images: Jon Arnold 4crb; Walter Bibikow 4cra; Nadia Isakova 4t; Ken Scicluna 2tr,3tl, 36-7, 64-5.

Belmond Grand Hotel Europe: Niall Clutton 59br.

Chesma Church: 103bl.

Clean Plate Society: Simkin Igor 76cla.

Corbis: 22cl, 23tl; Demotix/Mike Kireev 55cl; epa/Anatoly Maltsev 38br; Global Look/Photoagency Interpress 68c; Heritage Images 80cra; ITAR-TASS /Ruslan Shamukov 52cl, 54bc, 54t, /Denis Vyshinsky 54cl;Leemage 16tr.

Dreamstime.com: Sergei Afanasev 72tl; Aleks49 96cla; Alenmax 22br; Alexirina27000 21tl; Allexander 34-5; Anoli50 34cl; Arbiter 62b; Azurita 56cl; Befun 61tl; Alexandr Blinov 53b, 66tl; Irina Borsuchenko 34br; Tatiana Chepikova 79tr; Dance60 29crb; Olena Danileiko 57cla; Olga Demchishina 40t; Dimbar76 7t, 10br, 11tl, 11cr; Igor Dolgov 89t; Evgeny Drobzhev 92bl; Dvad 31tl; Elen33 26clb; Eugenesergeev 78tr; Evgeniy Fesenko 27tl; Iakov Filimonov 13br; Vladislav Gajic 44tl; Igor Groshev 7br, 32b; Afonskaya Irina 42cr; Anujak Jaimook 10tl; Joymsk 69b; Nikolai Korzhov 33cb; Andrey Koturanov 11tc, 35crb, 63cl; Veniamin Kraskov 60tl; Anton Kudelin 43t, 41cra; Pavel Lipskiy 14-5; Mazalis 60bc; Messiahphoto 12crb, 67br; Minadezhda 57clb; Vasily Mulyukin 11br; Anna Pakutina 13l; Pavel Parmenov 26ca; Pavelvasenkov 41bl; Natalia Pavlova 11cra; Ekaterina Pokrovsky 56tr, 75cla; Povarov 50tl; Andrei Rokhlov 50r; Romanevgenev 6b; Natalia Rumyantseva 31cra; Sailorr 28-9; Anton Samsonov 32cla; Sborisov 2tl, 6cl, 8-9, 101crb; Scaliger 18bl, 18-9, 30-1; Konstantin Semenov 27cr; German Sivov 40c; Nadezda Slobodinskaya 35tl; Aleksey Solodov 18cla, 29tl, 62tr, 88tl; Uatp1 63tr; Vitalyedush 28cla; 68-9, 86-7; Natalia Volkova 15t, 19tl; Gaspard Walter 61clb; Dmitriy Yakovlev 26-7; Ziashusha 57tr.

® Erarta: Vitaliy Kolikov 92tr.

iStockphoto.com: KateSmirnova 93c.

Getty Images: AFP/Olga Maltseva 49br; Panoramic Images 20-1; Harald Sund 10clb; White Night Press/Irina Bernstein/ullstein bild 21cr.

Jager Bar: KateSmirnova 93c.

Leningrad Zoo: 53tr.

Manhattan: 85br.

Mari Vanna: 58cl.

Mikhailovsky Theatre: 55tr.

Republic of Cats: 77tl.

Rex by Shutterstock: Lehtikuva Oy 39cl; Universal Images Group/Sovfoto 38t, / Universal History Archive 47clb.

Robert Harding Picture Library: Martin Child 4clb; Sylvain Grandadam 30br; Ferdinand Hollweck 90bl; Michael Nolan 74tl; Juergen Richter 80br; Ellen Rooney 24-5.

Romeo's Bar and Kitchen: Oleg Vaydner 83cb.

Russian Vodka Room No. 1: 59t.

Sadko: Yury Ermolov 83tl.

The State Hermitage Museum, St Petersburg: V.Terebenin, A.Terebenin 16bl, 17tl, 17crb, 90t; Vladimir Terebenin, Andrey Terebenin, Alexander Koksharov, Pavel Demidov 10cl, 14bl, 14br.

The State Museum of Political History of Russia: Stained Glass Window Of Vladimir Lenin by Artist A. Korolev 42bl.

Street Art Museum: *God at Work* by Roman Kreemos 51t.

SuperStock: Fine Art Images 46tl, 46cr, 47tl, / Brodski Museum/*Portrait of Vladimir Lenin* (1925) by Isaak Izrailevich Brodsky 39tr, /State Central Navy Museum, St. Petersburg painting by Alexander Alexandrovich Blinkov 44cr; Keystone Archives/Heritage-Images / Heritage 46bc.

Tsarskoye Selo Museum-Preserve: 4cla, 11clb, 33tl, 100tl, 102t.

Ukrop: 104bl.

W St. Petersburg: 77br.

Cover
Front and spine: **iStockphoto.com:** Iryna1

Back: **AWL Images:** Sylvain Sonnet tr; **Dreamstime.com:** Marcorubino crb; Mistervlad tl; Tomas1111 cla; **iStockphoto.com:** Iryna1

Pull Out Map Cover
iStockphoto.com: Iryna1

All other images © Dorling Kindersley
For further information see:
www.dkimages.com

As a guide to abbreviations in visitor information blocks: **Adm** = admission charge

Penguin Random House

Printed and bound in China

First edition 2008

Published in Great Britain by
Dorling Kindersley Limited
80 Strand, London WC2R 0RL

Published in the United States by
DK Publishing, 1450 Broadway,
8th Floor, New York, New York 10018

Copyright © 2008, 2019 Dorling
Kindersley Limited

A Penguin Random House Company

18 19 20 21 10 9 8 7 6 5 4 3 2 1

Reprinted with revisions 2010, 2012, 2014, 2017, 2019

A CIP catalogue record is available from the British Library.

A catalog record for this book is available from the Library of Congress.

ISSN 1479-344X

ISBN 978-0-2413-6468-0

MIX
Paper from
responsible sources
FSC
www.fsc.org   FSC™ C018179

Phrase Book

In this guide the Russian language has been transliterated into Roman script. All street and place names, and the names of most people, are transliterated according to this system. For some names, where a well-known English form exists, this has been used – hence, Leo (not Lev) Tolstoy. In particular, the names of Russian rulers, such as Peter the Great, are given in their anglicized forms. Throughout the book, transliterated names can be taken as an accurate guide to pronunciation. The Phrase Book also gives a phonetic guide to the pronunciation of words and phrases.

Guidelines for Pronunciation

The Cyrillic alphabet has 33 letters, of which only five (а, к, м, о, т) correspond exactly to their counterparts in English. Russian has two pronunciations (hard and soft) of each of its vowels, and several consonants without an equivalent. The right-hand column of the alphabet, below, demonstrates how Cyrillic letters are pronounced by comparing them to sounds in English words. However, some letters vary in how they are pronounced according to their position in a word. Important exceptions are also noted below. On the following pages, the English is given in the left-hand column, with the Russian and its transliteration in the middle column. But in the Menu Decoder section the Russian is given in the left-hand column and the English translation in the right-hand column, for ease of use. Because there are genders in Russian, in a few cases both masculine and feminine forms of a phrase are given.

THE CYRILLIC ALPHABET

А а	a	**a**limony
Б б	b	**b**ed
В в	v	**v**et
Г г	g	**g**et (see note 1)
Д д	d	**d**ebt
Е е	e	**ye**t (see note 2)
Ё ё	e	**yo**nder
Ж ж	zh	lei**s**ure (but a little harder)
З з	z	**z**ither
И и	i	s**ee**
Й й	y	bo**y** (see note 3)
К к	k	**k**ing
Л л	l	**l**oot
М м	m	**m**atch
Н н	n	**n**ever
О о	o	r**o**b (see note 4)
П п	p	**p**ea
Р р	r	**r**at (rolling, as in Italian)
С с	s	**s**top
Т т	t	**t**offee
У у	u	b**oo**t
Ф ф	f	**f**ellow
Х х	kh	**kh** (like loch)
Ц ц	ts	le**ts**
Ч ч	ch	**ch**air
Ш ш	sh	**sh**ove
Щ щ	shch	fre**sh sh**eet (with a slight roll)
ъ		hard sign (no sound, but see note 5)
Ы ы	y	l**i**d
ь		soft sign (no sound, but see note 5)
Э э	e	**e**gg
Ю ю	yu	**you**th
Я я	ya	**ya**k

Notes

1) Г Pronounced as v in endings -oro and -ero.
2) Е Always pronounced ye at the beginning of a word, but in the middle of a word sometimes less distinctly (more like e).
3) Й This letter has no distinct sound of its own. It usually lengthens the preceeding vowel.
4) О When not stressed it is pronounced like a in **a**cross.
5) ъ, ь The hard sign (ъ) is rare and indicates a very brief pause before the next letter. The soft sign (ь, marked in the pronunciation guide as ') softens the preceeding consonant and adds a slight y sound: for instance, n' would sound like ny in 'ca**ny**on'.

In an Emergency

Help!	Помогите! **Pomogite!**	pamageet-ye!
Stop!	Стоп! **Stop!**	stop!
Leave me alone!	Оставтье меня в покое! **Ostavte menya v pokoe!**	astavt'-ye myenya v pakoye!
Call a doctor!	Позовите врача! **Pozovite vracha!**	pazaveet-ye vracha!
Call an ambulance!	Вызовите скорую помощь! **Vyzovite skoruyu pomoshch!**	vizaveet-ye skoru-yu pomash!
Fire!	Пожар! **Pozhar!**	pazhar!
Police!	Полиция! **Politsiya!**	paleetsee-ya!
Where is the	Где **Gde**	gdye
nearest…	ближайший… **blizhayshiy…**	bleezhaysheey…
…telephone?	…телефон? **…telefon?**	…tyelyefon?
…hospital?	…больница? **…bolnitsa?**	…bal'neetsa?
…police station?	…отделение полиции? **…otdelenie politsii?**	…atdyelyenye paleetsee-ee?

Communication Essentials

Yes	Да **Da**	da
No	Нет **Net**	nyet
Please	Пожалуйста **Pozhaluysta**	pazhalsta
Thank you	Спасибо **Spasibo**	spaseeba
Excuse me	Извините **Izvinite**	eezveeneet-ye
Hello	Здравствуйте **Zdravstvuyte**	zdrastvooyt-ye
Goodbye	До свидания **Do svidaniya**	da sveedanya
What?	Что? **Chto?**	shto?
Where?	Где? **Gde?**	gdye?
Why?	Почему? **Pochemu?**	pachyemoo?
When?	Когда? **Kogda?**	kagda?

Useful Phrases

How are you?	Как Вы Поживаете? **Kak vee pozhivaete?**	kak vee pozhivaete?
Very well, thank you	Хорошо, спасибо **Khorosho, spaseeba**	kharasho, spaseeba
Pleased to meet you	Очень приятно **Ochen priyatno**	ochen' pree-yatna
How do I get to…?	Как добраться до…? **Kak dobratsya do…?**	kak dabrat'sya da…?
Do you speak English?	Вы говорите по-английски? **Vy govorite po-angliyskiy**	vi gavareet-ye po-angleeskee?
I don't understand	Я не понимаю **Ya ne ponimayu**	ya nye paneema-yoo
I am lost	я заблудился (заблудилась) **Ya zabludilsya (zabludilas)**	ya zabloodeelsya (zabloodeelas')

Useful Words

big	большой **bolshoy**	bal'shoy
small	маленький **malenkiy**	malyen'kee
hot (water, food)	горячий **goryachiy**	garyachee
hot (weather)	жарко **zharko**	zharka
cold	холодный **kholodnyy**	khalodnee
good	хорошо **khorosho**	kharasho
bad	плохо **plokho**	plokha
early	рано **rano**	rana
late	поздно **pozdno**	pozdna
free (no charge)	бесплатно **besplatno**	byesplatna
toilet	туалет **tualet**	tooalyet

Eating Out

I would like to book a table	Я хочу заказать стол **Ya khochu zakazat stol**	ya khachoo zakazat' stol
The bill, please	Счёт, пожалуйста **Schet, pozhaluysta**	shyot, pazhalsta
I am a vegetarian	Я вегетерианец (вегетерианка) **Ya vegeterianets (vegeterianka)**	ya vyegyetareeanyets (vyegyetareeanka)
breakfast	завтрак **zavtrak**	zaftrak
lunch	обед **obed**	abyet
dinner	ужин **uzhin**	oozheen
waiter!	официант! **ofitsiant!**	afeetsee-ant!

waitress!	официантка! **ofitsiantka!**	afeetsee-antka!
dish of the day	фирменное блюдо **firmennoe blyudo**	feermenoye blyooda
appetizers/ starters	закуски **zakuski**	zakooskee
main course	второе блюдо **vtoroe blyudo**	ftaroye blyooda
meat and poultry dishes	мясные блюда **myasnye blyuda**	myasniye blyooda
fish and seafood dishes	рыбные блюда **rybnye blyuda**	ribniye blyooda
vegetable dishes	овощные блюда **ovoshchnye blyuda**	avashshniye blyooda
dessert	десерт **desert**	dyesyert
drinks	напитки **napitki**	napeetkee
vegetables	овощи **ovoshchi**	ovashshee
bread	хлеб **khleb**	khlyeb
wine list	карта вин **karta vin**	karta veen
glass	стакан **stakan**	stakan
bottle	бутылка **butylka**	bootilka
salt	соль **sol**	sol'
pepper	перец **perets**	pyeryets
butter/oil	масло **maslo**	masla
sugar	сахар **sakhar**	sakhar

Menu Decoder

белое вино **beloe vino**	byelaye veeno	white wine
варёный **varenyy**	varyonee	boiled
вода **voda**	vada	water
жареный **zharenyy**	zharyenee	roasted/grilled/ fried
икра **ikra**	eekra	black caviar
икра красная/ кета **ikra krasnaya/ keta**	eekra krasna-ya/ kyeta	red caviar
красное вино **krasnoe vino**	krasnoye veeno	red wine
курица **kuritsa**	kooreetsa	chicken
лук **luk**	look	onion
минеральная вода **mineralnaya voda**	mineral'naya vada	mineral water
мясо **myaso**	myasa	meat
печёнка **pechenka**	pyechyonka	liver
печёный **pechenyy**	pyechyonee	baked

пиво **pivo**	*peeva*	beer
помидор **pomidor**	*pameedor*	tomato
морепродукты **moryeproduktee**	*moryeproduktee*	seafood
рыба **ryba**	*riba*	fish
салат **salat**	*salat*	salad
сосиски **sosiski**	*saseeskee*	sausages
сыр **syr**	*sir*	cheese
сырой **syroy**	*siroy*	raw
чеснок **chesnok**	*chyesnok*	garlic
яйцо **yaytso**	*yaytso*	egg
фрукты **frukty**	*frookti*	fruit

Staying in a Hotel

Do you have a vacant room?	У вас есть свободный номер? **U vas yest svobodnyy nomer?**	*oo vas yest' svabodnee nomyer?*
single room	одноместный номер **odnomestnyy nomer**	*adnamyestnee nomyer*
double room with double bed	номер с двуспальной кроватью **nomer s dvuspalnoy krovatyu**	*nomyer s dvoospal'noy kravat'-yoo*
key	ключ **klyuch**	*klyooch*

Time, Days and Dates

one minute	одна минута **odna minuta**	*adna meenoota*
one hour	час **chas**	*chas*
half an hour	полчаса **polchasa**	*polchasa*
day	день **den**	*dyen'*
week	неделя **nedelya**	*nyedyel-ya*
Monday	понедельник **ponedelnik**	*panyedyel'neek*
Tuesday	вторник **vtornik**	*ftorneek*
Wednesday	среда **sreda**	*sryeda*
Thursday	четверг **chetverg**	*chyetvyerk*
Friday	пятница **pyatnitsa**	*pyatneetsa*
Saturday	суббота **subbota**	*soobota*
Sunday	воскресенье **voskresene**	*vaskryesyen'ye*

Numbers

1	один/одна/одно **odin/odna/odno**	*adeen/adna/adno*
2	два/две **dva/dve**	*dva/dvye*
3	три **tri**	*tree*
4	четыре **chetyre**	*chyetir-ye*
5	пять **pyat**	*pyat'*
6	шесть **shest**	*shest*
7	семь **sem**	*syem*
8	восемь **vosem**	*vosyem'*
9	девять **devyat**	*dyevyat'*
10	десять **desyat**	*dyesyat'*
11	одиннадцать **odinnadtsat**	*adeenatsat'*
12	двенадцать **dvenadtsat**	*dvyenatsat'*
13	тринадцать **trinadtsat**	*treenatsat'*
14	четырнадцать **chetyrnadtsat**	*chyetirnatsat'*
15	пятнадцать **pyatnadtsat**	*pyatnatsat'*
16	шестнадцать **shestnadtsat**	*shestnatsat'*
17	семнадцать **semnadtsat**	*syemnatsat'*
18	восемнадцать **vosemnadtsat**	*vasyemnatsat'*
19	девятнадцать **devyatnadtsat**	*dyevyatnatsat'*
20	двадцать **dvadtsat**	*dvatsat'*
30	тридцать **tridtsat**	*treetsat'*
40	сорок **sorok**	*sorak*
50	пятьдесят **pyatdesyat**	*pyadyesyat'*
60	шестьдесят **shestdesyat**	*shes'dyesyat*
70	семьдесят **semdesyat**	*syem'dyesyat*
80	восемьдесят **vosemdesyat**	*vosyem'dyesyat*
90	девяносто **devyanosto**	*dyevyanosta*
100	сто **sto**	*sto*
200	двести **dvesti**	*dvyestee*
300	триста **trista**	*treesta*
400	четыреста **chetyresta**	*chyetiryesta*
500	пятьсот **pyatsot**	*pyat'sot*
1,000	тысяча **tysyacha**	*tisyacha*
2,000	две тысячи **dve tysyachi**	*dvye tisyachi*
5,000	пять тысяч **pyat tysyach**	*pyat' tisyach*
1,000,000	миллион **million**	*meelee-on*